the Way of the Voice of Peace

RICH MARANTZ

SHIRES PRESS

4869 Main Street
P.O. Box 2200
Manchester Center, VT 05255
www.northshire.com/printondemand

the Way of the Voice of Peace

Editing: Lynne Putnam, Joy Frank, Elizabeth Perry
Cover art: Donna Oliver
Inside illustration: Jade Marantz
Book design: Debbi Wraga
Technical support and photography: Lorrie Marantz

For additional work by Rich visit:
www.greenmountaintaichi.com

ISBN Number: 978-1-60571-098-3
Library Of Congress Number: 2011900001

Building Community, One Book at a Time
This book was printed at the Northshire Bookstore, a family-owned,
independent bookstore in Manchester Ctr., Vermont, since 1976.
We are committed to excellence in bookselling.
The Northshire Bookstore's mission is to serve as a resource for
information, ideas, and entertainment while honoring the needs of
customers, staff, and community.

Printed in the United States of America

Acknowledgements

Throughout this book, the telling of my experiences are just that, my experiences. While I have done my best to portray situations and conversations accurately, those with whom I have shared the experiences I describe may perceive them slightly or even very differently. I can only hope that I honor them, as I am truly appreciative of and grateful for the role they have played in my life.

Tremendous effort and countless hours were put into the writing and production of this book and it could not have been accomplished without the encouragement, wisdom, and effort of the following people:

Lorrie, Jade, Master Yun Xiang Tseng (Chen), the Carthusians at the Charterhouse of the Transfiguration, Lynne, Donna, Elizabeth, Kevin, Mary Louise, Katya, Joy, Rueben, Kristina, Dwight, Nanatasis, all of my students, friends, and those who inadvertently taught me along the way.

Dedicated To:

Lorrie and Jade for their unending belief in me.
Master Yun Xiang Tseng (Chen)
for guiding me so I may find my purpose.
Spirit for the message and motivating energy
required to write this book.

CONTENTS

Peace through the eyes of a child.

PREPARATION

Truth lies not merely in words.
Truth lies within the energy of peace.
We can name the energy of peace, love.
-Rich Marantz

When beginning a journey, it is ideal to start off on stable ground with a firm footing. However, at times our journeys begin in the turmoil of everyday life. So, whether you are on firm ground or in turmoil, let us begin.

This book relates the story of my personal journey from a point of near despair to a place of inner peace. The peace I am referring to is a state in which we see with clarity our own original nature. It is a loving state that provides us with a deep sense of tranquility and stillness, in which we feel and express our intimate link with Spirit and humanity. With it comes a genuine happiness that does not fluctuate with the ups and downs of our often roller coaster-like lives.

There is a process each one of us must go through to reveal the experience of peace that resides within. The personal incidents, lessons, and turning points I share reveal how I came to understand and act upon core insights at various points along my path. Although the process and order of insights will vary for each individual, there are some basic perceptions and behaviors that facilitate our movement towards peace. A few of the lessons I learned along the way include becoming comfortable with stillness and silence, understanding and detaching from the games of ego, giving and receiving kindness, remaining focused in the present moment, and remaining disciplined in my commitment to a daily practice of Tai chi, meditation, and prayer. Anchoring these ways of being helped me awaken to an alternative way of viewing life in general and my life in particular. In the process, I moved closer to my authentic self.

Although this book tells my story, it is not

really about me or any of the other people with whom I have had the great fortune to cross paths. Nor does the message I share originate with me. It is a message from Spirit, told through me to guide you, the reader, to find the voice of peace within your own life. I am simply a conduit.

An implied message which runs throughout the book is that you do not have to live in a cloistered religious community or have special credentials to achieve a state of inner calm and self-acceptance. If I were to have any letters after my name, they wouldn't be M.D. or Ph.D.; they would be J.S.G. for "just some guy." I am an ordinary person, who started from a place of emotional turmoil and incapacitating physical pain, but managed to discover a path to peace while immersed in the many mundane moments and frequent challenges of an everyday life.

Who is this book for? Basically it is for anyone who knows, deep down, that living a life of chasing outside for what already resides within is futile. It is also for those who are sick and tired of feeling sick and tired. Above all, this book is for all of us who are willing to take the journey of tapping into our fullest human potential and true nature by returning our focus to the source of our being. It is a story of awakening and renewal, told through the eyes of an average guy who is nonetheless disciplined, dedicated, and devoted to finding peace and the fulfillment that goes with it.

Throughout this book, I use the terms *God*, *Spirit*, *Creator*, *Divine*, and *Tao* when speaking of the sacred. I do not do so to be politically correct or to cover my bases. I also do not use them due to any confusion on my part. Rather, I use a variety of words, because putting a singular name to what I am describing always seems to fall short, and I prefer to use whatever term best fits the context of whatever story I am telling in the moment.

A term that appears frequently is the Chinese word, *Tao*, which translates as the way or path. There are many subtleties to its meaning, however. Tao is what was before all that is. It is also what permeates and describes the particular nature of all that is. As Lao Tzu writes in the first chapter of the *Tao Te Ching*:

The Tao that can be told is not the eternal Tao.

The name that can be named is not the eternal name.

The nameless is the beginning of heaven and earth.

The named is the mother of the ten thousand things.

What I intend in writing this book is to describe my direct experience with that which cannot be described. I may use form in the way of words and sentences, but it is the formless and its relationship to the formed which I am attempting to reveal. Peace, after all, is not a thing; it is an experience, and whatever situation or lesson I am describing is likely to capture only one aspect of what I seek to portray overall.

One of my favorite tales illustrates this point. There was once a king who had many spiritual advisors. Each advisor claimed to have the answers to the problems we all face in this lifetime. Each one claimed to know the truth, and each vied for the attention of the king. Each tried to prove that only his way was right. One day the king tired of all the arguing among his different advisors and the chaos that it brought about, so he called everyone together and asked that an elephant, along with four blind men, be brought before them. The advisors looked at each other with a mixture of confusion and amusement. The king then asked the first blind man to approach the elephant, touch it, and tell him what it looked like. The blind man touched the leg of the elephant and said, "King, the elephant looks like a tree trunk." The king then asked the same of the next blind man, who touched the side of the elephant and said, "King, the elephant looks like a wall." The king then summoned the third blind man to do the same. He touched the elephant's tail and declared, "King, this elephant looks like a rope." The fourth blind man touched the trunk and said, "King, the elephant looks like a large snake." The king then turned to his advisors, who were very confused, and said to them, "All of these blind men are right, yet none of them are *all* right."

In the telling of this story, I am speaking my truth, which I have been called by Spirit to share. It is my sincere hope that my experiences and words will be of use to you in finding your greater purpose, your own truth, and peace.

Chapter 1

DIVINE VOICE

We have what we seek, it is there all the time,
and if we give it time, it will make itself known to us.
-Thomas Merton

The summer I was 11 years old my family took a boat trip to Beach Haven, New Jersey. On that trip I came down with a severe bout of tonsillitis, which was a condition that plagued me throughout childhood. This time, as I was alone on the boat and my parents were out to dinner, my throat swelled to such an extent I could hardly breathe and I began to run a very high fever. Lying on my bunk in the bow, my fever escalated, I was in extreme pain, vomiting, and having trouble breathing. I knew I was in trouble but did not know what to do to help myself.

It was then I heard an inner voice for the first time in my life. *"Get up. Go get help."* The tone was loving yet firm enough that I took action. Even though I was delirious with fever, I somehow managed to get out of my bunk, off our boat, and onto the dock, where I spotted some people sitting nearby on their back deck, enjoying a summer evening. I must have been a pitiful sight as I approached them, drenched in sweat and covered in vomit. "I need help," I whispered. Fortunately the woman I approached happened to be a nurse, and she did, indeed, provide me with the assistance I needed, for which I will be forever grateful. Someone located my parents and I was taken to the hospital for treatment, after which I recovered within a few days.

The memory of the inner voice which guided me to seek help that day was never far from my conscious mind, although a year would pass before I would hear it once again. This time, however, I would recognize it. Same voice, same scenario. Take action or you may die.

It happened the following summer, during another boat trip my family took on the *Sea Six*, our 38-foot Colonial cabin cruiser. The *Sea Six* was a really cool boat, with teak decks and lots of character. My parents had owned it throughout my childhood, and as a result I grew to love everything about boating and being on the water, including fishing and swimming.

Our route on this trip took us, as it did the previous summer, through Barnegat Bay and the inland waterway to the island town of Beach Haven, New Jersey, where we docked at a marina on the bay side. From there it was just a quarter mile walk to the Atlantic Ocean. This was summer on the Jersey shore – which meant ice cream, kites, saltwater taffy, beach play, crabbing, and fishing. What a great place for a bold and active 12 year-old boy!

On this particular trip we were accompanied by another boat, which was owned by my parent's oldest friends, whom I referred to as my aunt and uncle, and whose children I referred to as cousins. One day I went to the ocean with my slightly older cousin to go bodysurfing, which is an art, as well as a skill and a whole lot of fun. However, you have to be willing to swallow a lot of seawater and sand. You also have to be willing to end up with a bucket of sand in your shorts, or maybe even lose your shorts. The technique used is identical to regular surfing, with the exception that your body becomes the board. Basically, you swim out to where the waves are breaking, swim as fast as you can to "catch the wave," then put your arms straight out in front, stiffen your whole body like a board, and ride the wave into the beach. YeeeHaaa!!!

On this particular day the waves were high, the ocean rough, and the tide strong. Although there were many people on the beach, few were swimming due to these conditions. Not me, I was going to ride these monster waves (at least that is the way they appeared through the eyes of a young boy). I dove in and was having a great time, when along came the biggest wave of all. This was going to be great, I thought. I began swimming as fast as I could, when I felt a tremendous force crash down upon me. I knew right away I would not be riding this wave to the beach.

Its power forced me headfirst into the hard sandy bottom, and I was knocked unconscious. In this state, I was seeing the whole scene as if watching a movie in a totally darkened theater. I saw, from a distance, my body fold in half backward as it was being tossed around by the turbulence. Yet there was no pain… only blackness, quiet, and my body being played with by the immense power of the ocean. It was then that I heard the voice. *"Get up and run,"* it said. There was only blackness, quiet, and my body. *"Get up and run,"* the voice said again. There was a soothing quality about it, without any sense of rush or panic, and yet it grabbed my attention.

I awoke to sheer terror, not knowing which way was up, down, or sideways within the extreme turbulence of water that surrounded me in all directions. I could not breathe, and my lungs were screaming for air. Once again, the loving but firm voice directed me: *"Get up and run."* This time I obeyed. Inexplicably my feet hit bottom, and I began running. How I knew from under water which way was up, let alone which direction to head in for shore, I still cannot say, but as I emerged from the water, I found myself moving toward the safety of dry land. When I made it to shallow water, I collapsed, unable to move, as waves washed in and out over my body.

I was aware of my cousin running to the lifeguard stand about 30 feet away. I watched him, as if watching a movie. He was trying to convince the lifeguard I was hurt and needed help, but the lifeguard took little notice until a crowd had gathered around me. (Looking back, I cannot help but think that lifeguard was in the wrong line of work.) To this day, I remember with immense gratitude the group of men who rescued me. Working as a team, they gently lifted my motionless body and carried me onto dry sand.

By then the rescue squad had arrived. They put me on a stiff backboard, which is used to immobilize patients with a potential spinal injury, and someone went to the marina to tell my parents. My mother and I were taken to a shore hospital and then transported the 80 miles or so to a hospital near my hometown. Beyond that my memory is of way too many lonely days and nights in a hospital bed, unable to get up, then of going home to endless days of constantly wearing a very uncomfortable and smelly back brace. In time my body and spine recovered, although I still have a few minor physical reminders of that accident. It would be 12 years before I could bring myself to swim in the ocean again.

So where did the voice come from that guided me as I was in danger of drowning that day? Some would say it came from my unconscious and some would say it was my imagination. I don't think so. From the moment I heard that voice until this day I believe it was Divine intervention. Whose actual voice it was guiding me into action, I have no idea. What I do know is the source of that voice came from beyond this physical world, which awakened in me an unwavering faith and belief in God.

In retrospect, this experience with Divine voice was one of the primary reasons I did not continue, after the age of thirteen, in the religion of my birth. I had never felt the presence of God in the temple, where it seemed He was only talked about. I was not satisfied, though, with just knowing about God in theory. I was seeking an experiential relationship with God, who mercifully guided me out of darkness and confusion on that fateful day.

Chapter 2

THE SEARCH BEGINS

Sometimes what we see as special
is actually very ordinary.
Sometimes what we see as ordinary
is actually very special.
It is within us to see beyond the illusion.
-Rich Marantz

In the years following the two traumatic events in which a Divine voice guided me out of danger, I felt disconnected from the physical world in which I lived. I had received a glimpse of God's immense love, but during my teenage years, this level of understanding was beyond me. I felt adrift, with no idea how I could build on my brief encounter with divinity, even though I desperately wanted to bring harmony and unconditional love into my fragmented life, which was anything but peaceful.

After my experience with Divine voice, I began to experiment with various ways of bridging the gap between our physical and non-physical worlds. Certainly there are many ways to tap into a non-physical reality, which can appear in many forms. With proper training, this can be done safely and in ways that profoundly benefit those walking a spiritual path. However, even beginners, without formal training, can happen into the realm of the non-physical worlds. The following story tells of one occasion where the unexpected occurred, and the unknown was revealed.

It was approximately two years after my near-drowning accident, and I was lying in bed at my home in suburban northern New Jersey. Although I did not name it as such at the time, I was meditating. On this particular occasion, the longer I meditated, the lighter I felt. I was aware of my body, but was feeling it less and less as the minutes went by. Suddenly I felt myself lift out of my body and flip over in an energy body (I did not call it this at the time), which was a mirror image to my physical body. Both were lying down on their backs, touching each other at the top of the head. As I continued to lie on my bed, the energy body began to rise upward in the room. I was still very aware of my physical body, but had no physical sensations. Then I found myself fully in the energy body, floating near the ceiling of our living room, looking down at my parents. My father was sitting on the couch, my mother across from him in a chair; both of them were reading a newspaper.

After an unknown amount of time, I returned to my physical body, opened my eyes and tried to make sense of what had just occurred. I walked into the living room and confirmed that, sure enough, my parents were sitting reading the newspaper, exactly as my energy body had witnessed. I stood there for a moment, turned around and went back to my room without saying a word, desperately wanting to know what had just happened to me.

I had not searched long when I discovered a book on the phenomenon of astral projection. Now at least I had a name and explanation for what I had experienced. After reading about some of the ways one can consciously leave the body during astral projection, I began to experiment with some of the techniques. However, all of my efforts at the time failed.

In retrospect, there are two reasons I am glad I was unable to develop the skill of astral travel. The first is that had I been able to travel out of my body at will, I would more than likely have enjoyed it too much and played with it to the detriment of my everyday life. In a manner of speaking, I might have lost touch with my physical reality, which was already tenuous at best. This was partly due to the fact that, as a young child, I had been subjected to a hidden life of abuse to the body and mind, and as a result, I often felt afraid, ignored, alone, and haunted by the belief that I held no value as a human being. My guess is that had I been able to recreate my experience with astral travel, this would only have added to my psychological instability.

My second reason for being glad that my teenage efforts at astral projection failed is best conveyed by an anecdote told to me by a Lakota friend who facilitated sweat lodge ceremonies I attended regularly for two years of my adult life. On one occasion I shared with my friend that I had received several invitations to other sweat lodges, but declined all but one, because although I liked the people who extended these invitations, I did not trust them sufficiently to open myself within a ceremony they facilitated.

My wise friend responded by telling of an incident, which I refer to often in my teaching. "When I was a little boy," he said, "my brother and I got into the car in our driveway. We started the car, put it into gear, backed out of the driveway, and proceeded to crash the car right into a tree." We both let out a deep belly laugh, him at the memory, me at the image. "Anyone, even a child," he continued, "can start a car and get it going, but it doesn't mean they can steer or stop." He went on to say that connecting with spirit is not a game. One must be sincere and know what to do once things get going.

Throughout my teenage years I remained intrigued by the fact that there is more to us than our physical bodies and more to this world than what we can see, touch, feel, hear, and smell, but I didn't know what to do with that awareness or my curiosity. Unfortunately, there was no spiritual guidance available to help me understand and cultivate my connection with the Divine during that period of my life, and so I was left to my own devices. I spent many years searching and experimenting blindly.

Without guidance, I began to drift away from being connected to, and being able to hear Divine voice. Instead I turned to drugs and alcohol as a means of allowing me to temporarily leave my body and connect with the non-physical reality. As a young man I sought to alleviate my ever present fear and self-loathing, and gain power by experimenting with various dark forces, through reading books and attempting ways to play with those energies. Needless to say, these efforts served only as a distraction, which had the effect of intensifying my pain and leading me away from the love and peace I craved.

This continued until a turning point came when I experienced a crisis in my mid-twenties, which brought me to a crossroads of great significance on my search for inner peace. This would lead me back onto my path, where I would then have the good fortune to receive numerous teachers and guides, both in the physical and metaphysical world.

Chapter 3

HEALING

Happiness is not something ready-made.
It comes from your own actions.
-Dalai Lama

Sometimes it seems I need to be hit on the head with a brick, so to speak, before undergoing transformation in my life. Certainly the most significant turning point of my life was born out of trauma.

I was 27 years old at the time, working in a print shop in Clearwater, Florida. One day I attempted to help three other guys lift a 500-pound printing press off a pallet. "One, two, three, lift!" The problem was

I lifted, but the others didn't. As my end of the press came off the pallet, an audible *pop* came from my lower back. I knew I was hurt. What I did not know was that I would not work again for ten months, or that, more importantly, I was about to embark on a path of physical, psychological, emotional, and spiritual healing. With that pop in my back, an incredibly difficult yet rewarding journey commenced, from which there would be no turning back.

Two months after my accident, I underwent surgery to remove the disc that had been severely ruptured in my lower back. The surgery was unsuccessful, however, and I lived in constant unbearable pain, despite taking strong pain medications, which had the effect of turning my mind to jelly. The only time I left the house was for doctors' appointments, only to hear that I would have to learn to live with intense pain. The doctors also predicted I would have arthritis in my spine within five years due to the removal of the injured disc. Fortunately, they were wrong on both counts!

After sliding downhill for many long months, I enrolled in a three-week inpatient pain management program for people living with chronic pain. During my initial meeting with the physician at that program, he told me that I looked like a pretzel, because my posture had been distorted from muscle spasms which I suffered throughout my entire body. Here I was, 27 years old, with the posture of a 90 year-old man, and an unhealthy one at that.

A few days into my stay, while meeting with one of the staff, I found myself crying. This was not something I was prone to, and at that time, certainly not in front of a stranger. I told her it was because the pain was so severe. What I did not say, mostly because I did not understand it, was that it was emotional pain, rather than physical pain, that was bringing me to tears.

In the course of this pain management program, I learned three very important lessons. The first lesson, which came through the use of meditation and biofeedback, was that I could use mind to control my body. Biofeedback literally showed me that my muscles would respond to a simple change in mindset. If I was uptight, my muscles would tense and spasm, but if I calmed down by regulating my mind, my muscles would relax some. The biofeedback machine I was wired to illustrated this response with either colored lines or varying size boxes displayed on a TV screen. The relationship between my mental and emotional state and the degree of rigidity or relaxation in my muscles was unmistakable.

In addition, I received my first formal training in meditation. I was taught to scan through my body, becoming aware of any tension, and then to purposely direct my thoughts to release that tension. Like biofeedback, this technique proved effective in controlling and minimizing the whole-body muscle spasms. It also served as a formal introduction to the practice of meditation, which I have continued to this day.

My second lesson was that attitude is a determining factor in what we experience and its outcome. This became evident to me, as I observed that some people who came into our rehabilitation program in wheelchairs were able to walk out, while others who came in using canes, left using canes. What made the difference was their attitude, including what they expected to get out of the program and the effort they put into it. The ones who walked out knew they had a central role to play in their healing process and were not looking for someone else to fix them. Today I often teach in my Tai chi and Qigong classes that no matter how effective a healing method is thought to be, you are the most important ingredient. It is your intention and actions that unlock whatever potential a given therapy holds. Of course, those who facilitate and guide us in our recovery play a crucial role, but like the methods we choose, they simply help us to help ourselves. If our attitude is negative, we will be unable to clearly see the assistance and encouragement that is being offered. However, if we maintain hope, and a sincere desire to restore ourselves to health, the likelihood is that all the support we need will appear, seemingly at the right place at the right time.

The third lesson I learned in the pain management program was that my problems went much deeper than the physical. With the help of psychotherapy sessions, I began to unravel the effects my past had on my then present state of being. This was by no means a quick process, but true healing, I could see, required me to address far more than the physical symptoms of my injury.

I left the pain management program with a

hopeful attitude and some very useful tools to aid in my recovery and healing. "I can do this!" I told myself. However, my life was still a train wreck. I remained in constant physical pain, and while I had taken myself off all prescription pain medications prior to entering the program, once I got home I replaced them with illicit street drugs. I told myself I was taking them to help with the muscle spasms, but even then I knew I was fooling myself. My primary emotions seemed limited to anger and indifference, and my turning to drugs was an attempt to cover up and make more tolerable this unacceptable way of being.

I was once again going downhill fast – unable to work, in constant physical pain and severely depressed. I was suffering and wanted out. Each day, I would hope and ask for this to be my last day on earth. I even went so far as to make several covert phone calls to a suicide hotline. Something had to change to take me off this steep slope I was quickly sliding down, and the first sign of a shift came in the form of work.

This was a perfect entry point for change in my life, because both of my parents had worked very hard throughout my life and instilled in me, through example, an incredibly strong work ethic. This served me well so long as I was able to work, because it was ingrained in me to be reliable and to perform to the best of my ability while on the job. There was a flip side to this strong work ethic, however, which revealed itself when I was sitting at home, disabled by pain and unable to hold down a job. Since, in the past, I had relied on work for my identity, in my mind the loss of my ability to work translated as a loss of who I was. I believed I was no longer of any use, so why bother to exist? Each day, as I watched my wife go off to work, I would sink deeper into depression and self-deprecation. I knew that if I was to survive, I had to find a way to get back to work.

The insurance company that was handling my case offered to retrain me, since I could no longer handle the physical demands of my former job in printing. I located and enrolled in a program to learn how to make and repair jewelry, subsequently landing a part-time job as an apprentice bench jeweler. Working part-time work was ideal, because at this point in my recovery, the pain I experienced was still too intense to allow working a full day.

Going back to work lifted my spirits. Once again I was bringing home a paycheck, and I was happy to be learning a new skill which not only involved creatively working with my hands, but also provided me with a way out of the printing industry, in which I no longer wanted to work.

Another turning point came when, in addition to the pain I endured throughout my body, I developed a chronic headache that lasted about a month. It was obvious to me that conventional therapies were not helping the pain in either my back or head, so I decided to try acupuncture and herbs. After about three weeks on this regimen, my headache disappeared. Intrigued, I thought there must be something to this, so I went to the library (this was pre-Internet) to read about alternative healing. One of the books I explored was about Chinese medicine and contained a section on Tai chi chuan, a Chinese martial and healing art. This captured my interest, and I asked my acupuncturist if he knew of anyone teaching Tai chi. Fortunately, he had a flier advertising an instructor in Tampa, Florida, about an hour's drive from my home.

Initially my interest in Tai chi as a form of therapy

was because it is a martial art. Back then I was a self-proclaimed tough guy, who believed yoga (the other option) was for girls. In addition, I had been a wrestler from the time I was a very young child and always found myself drawn to the fighting arts. The two-hour round trip to my lesson was torturous, because each bounce of the car sent a bolt of pain into my still healing spine. However, I loved Tai chi from my very first lesson, so I endured the pain.

I began this component of my journey by taking a private class once a week. At each lesson, my teacher would lead me through a gentle Qigong (energy exercise) warm-up, and then proceed to teach me three new moves out of the 108 movements I would eventually learn. First thing each morning, I would go out onto the pool deck behind my house to practice what I had learned. In addition, I would often practice in the pool itself, as the buoyancy of the water, combined with the movements, offered some pain relief.

For three years I practiced *every single day* without a break. What motivated me to do this was simple; whenever I would practice my Tai chi movements, the pain I was used to experiencing was either not present or not as severe, and with each passing day the positive effects of practice lasted a few minutes more than the day before. After three years of consistent disciplined practice, the pain which had plagued me diminished to the point where it was no longer the central focus of my life. After seven years of practicing *every single day,* I would experience pain only if I placed excessive strain on my lower back. After ten years, pain was no longer an issue in my life. Since then I have continued with a daily practice of Tai chi, and over the course of two decades, I have accumulated no more than a month or two of missed practice days.

During this time, I began to learn the concepts which accompany a Tai chi and Qigong practice, such as the importance of emphasizing consistency and quality of effort above quantity and the value of placing more emphasis on the substance of what I was doing than on the way things appeared. I started to incorporate these teachings into my life in general, as each day I spent time pondering the philosophy of Tai chi, in addition to practicing the physical movements. This process, although certainly worthwhile, required an immense amount of effort on my part. As the late Master Jou, Tsung Hwa was fond of saying, "It's simple, not easy. Tai chi is hard work."

Chapter 4
RELEASING AND LETTING GO

If people realized they are loved as they are,
then they want to begin to change.
-Jean Varnier

I was making slow but steady progress by practicing Tai chi each day and working part-time as a jeweler, yet something was still not right. I felt as if I had a dark pit in my stomach. I didn't know what the problem was, but I knew I couldn't take feeling this way any longer. Later I discovered that some of what I was experiencing – regular night terrors, indifference, excessive anger, and a feeling that I was fragmented – were textbook symptoms of post-traumatic stress disorder and clinical depression.

Eventually I made the connection between this dark feeling in the pit of my stomach and the secret that I carried deep within, which I swore I would take to my grave. As I reached the point where I could no longer endure my life as it was, I knew I must tell my wife, Lorrie, my secret: that I had been sexually and physically abused as a child. I dreaded admitting this to her, because I actually thought she would not want anything to do with me once she knew. Thankfully she responded in the best possible way, with a hug and understanding.

It was then I could begin the next phase of healing on my path to peace: learning to release and let go of old psychological wounds. About two years after beginning the practice of Tai chi, I took another major step by going to a talented therapist, who guided me in seeing objectively what I had experienced as a child. This was not an easy or pleasant process for someone as closed and disconnected from self as I was. However, the process of emotional healing was helped along by the lessons I was absorbing while healing my body with a daily routine of Tai chi and Qigong.

In some ways I feel most of us deal with post-traumatic stress disorder simply because we are living in a muddy world, a world that is impure. Not one of us gets through this life without scars of some sort. It is only in the degree of severity in which we differ. In addition, events which appear to lie at the origin of our pain are not the only factor in the way we carry these experiences into our lives. If they were, then two people who experience identical events would have the same reaction and response. A factor which I believe plays a large role in whether we feel traumatized or not is whether or not we stay *present* while the event is happening. However, when we are unaware, this is not always possible.

Through years of receiving physical, philosophical, traditional healing and spiritual training, and then cultivating these teachings through practice, I have come to understand how the traumatic events of my childhood informed my actions as an adult. As a child I could not stay present when I was subjected to physical and sexual abuse. What was occurring during those events was intolerable, so my spirit would leave my body. In addition, my child's mind could not adequately process and understand what my body was experiencing, which left my body to go through the experience alone. This results in the setting of a body memory because my mind, which could not comprehend what was happening, activated physical energy which in turn collected and formed within my body without any awareness of my mind. When I would have future experiences that were not even directly related to the abuse, it would trigger the body memory, and release the stored energy that had been trapped within my body. Since my spirit and mind were not present when the memory was set, the energy that would be released at these times was not familiar or even recognizable, so I would react *mindlessly* and focus blame for my inappropriate actions on the trigger, rather than my own buried emotions.

As a teenager, this dynamic would be played out often when I would attend parties or concerts. The whole time I would be on high alert, knowing that at some point someone would touch or bump into me. (I was well into adulthood before I felt comfortable allowing anyone to touch me.) When the inevitable happened, I would react with anger and yell, "What do you think you are doing?" At times, I would physically confront whoever bumped me, while subconsciously thinking, "Why are you doing this to me?" During these episodes, I put all my focus on what the other person was doing to me and how I could get them to change, so I would no longer be angry. As long as my focus remained outside myself, however, the situation escalated. Of course, this did nothing to take care of the root problem, and I was in a constant state of conflict. The problem was not that someone bumped into me, but rather that old memory buttons were being pushed within me.

It is common in our society to say, "That person is pushing my buttons." We can think of these buttons as connected to sensitive areas within us, such as places of fear, low self-esteem, or doubt that stem from emotional trauma and unfulfilled need. Those who know us well, such as a spouse, sibling, or parent, know exactly which buttons to push and when to push them to fulfill some need or agenda of their own, even if they are not consciously aware of what they are doing. Of course, this works the other way around as well; we also know which buttons to push on others. When we are caught in this game of having our buttons pushed or pushing another's buttons, we are in a state of mindless conflict, and in such a state, needless to say, we are unable to realize peace.

If we can learn to be *mindful* in our response, however, this opens the way to peace. Instead of behaving like a victim by pointing the finger outward in blame, we can turn our awareness inward to disengage from and release old stored energy, so that others can no longer subconsciously control us. It takes courage, though, to look at old wounds and adhere to a commitment of peace being your primary goal.

I once attended a lecture in which an enlightened Taoist master made the following statement: "The only difference between me and you is that I have let go of my garbage and each day I get rid of any new garbage." The garbage he was referring to is the false information that has been impressed upon us throughout our lives that we have taken as truth. An example of this would be if, as a child, you were told you were worthless; then, as an adult, you carry with you the belief that you are worthless, and it becomes the basis of your actions and decisions. This dynamic is something each one of us experiences, because those who nurture us while we are developing are often carrying their own garbage, and they interact with us based on their belief in their own false truths. Instead of focusing blame on what someone else has done to us, we can simply recognize it, so we do not unconsciously dump our garbage onto others.

How do we get past this game of someone pushing our buttons and us reacting as a victim instead of responding with purposeful choice? After years of healing psychological wounds and letting go of emotional garbage, I have learned that whenever I am in a difficult situation, I want my first action to be one of turning inward, so I can be mindful in my response. To accomplish this, my first step is to ask myself, "How do I feel?"

What I then do with that awareness may appear counterintuitive to our cultural upbringing: I do nothing. Often our reaction is to figure out what is going on and why we feel the way we do; then we focus on changing it. But do we really need to know what something is to let it go? I believe it is much simpler than that: *Release and let go first; know later.*

My process for releasing is simple, but not

easy. Once I recognize what it is that I am feeling in a given situation, whether pleasant or unpleasant, I focus on letting go of the urge to change it. *Accepting what is* can be a challenge, but I have come to understand that to bring about inner transformation, we must fully accept the way we feel at any given moment, without any desire to alter that feeling. It is through this unconditional love and acceptance of who we are that we will begin to act in a way that is conducive to change.

Now I am ready to ask myself a second question: "Why am I doing what I am doing?" In other words, what is really motivating my actions and reactions? When I first began asking myself this question, it was to know in each situation whether my intentions were of pure heart or to fulfill some deep-seated ego need. Were my actions for the good of all involved, or did I have an agenda I was looking to meet? Let me give an example. One day my wife and I were having a conversation about some remodeling I had done on our house that was not to her liking. The conversation soon became heated, and instead of resolving our differences, the divide between us was widening, and we were becoming increasingly angry. In the midst of this, I stopped talking, took the time to pay attention to my breathing, how I was feeling, and why I was saying what I was saying. I soon realized that arguing my point had nothing to do with whether the project needed to be done again. Rather, I had an agenda, which was to feel appreciated for the work I had completed. At that point I was able to receive my wife's viewpoint as valid, instead of perceiving it as an attack on me, and to respond in a mindful instead of a defensive manner.

The practice of mindful response has provided me with the foundation of a life principle: to hold and apply the intention that everyone involved in a situation leaves the situation feeling right - not "right" as in right or wrong, but right in the sense of feeling aligned and comfortable within our own skin. If we take this approach, we begin to empathize with our fellow man, because we see that all of us, at some time or another, are reacting to the energy of old wounds and as a result, judging either ourselves or others. When we truly grasp this, we are able to move in the direction of forgiveness for self, as well as others. We are then able to move from seeing ourselves as victims of our life to being peaceful with, and accepting, whatever comes our way and whatever we are feeling.

Chapter 5

CHINA

When we know enough is enough,
we will always be happy.
-Taoist saying

In the late summer of 2001, I spent two months in China. My purpose for traveling there was to study and train in the Chinese internal martial, healing, and meditative arts, as well as to learn the Chinese language and culture. What I could not foresee was that a significant lesson of this trip would come in the form of a sincere demonstration of love and compassion.

For the majority of my visit, I stayed at Tian

Long Gong, (Heavenly Dragon Palace) a martial and healing arts training and retreat center located in the mountains about two hours from the city of Chengdu, in Sichuan province. Tian Long Gong was across a valley from Qing Cheng Mountain, a small yet important center of Taoism, where a huge 1800-year-old gingko tree is said to have been planted by Zhang Dao Ling, founder of the Taoist religion.

The training and daily regimen at Tian Long Gong was intense and vigorous. There was plenty of time, however, to integrate all that I was learning, since the pace of our routine was slow and steady. Each morning, beginning at 6:00 a.m., we would practice Tai chi and Qigong until breakfast at 8:00. We then attended two more hours of martial arts training before lunch, followed by two more hours of classes and training before dinner, then two more hours of classes and meditation before bedtime. In between training sessions we would eat, relax, write, go hiking on a mountain trail, or walk a mile down to the river for a swim. At times we would simply hang out and I would practice my Chinese, while helping other residents at the center practice their English. It was a hot and humid summer of living a simple country life. Two other Americans were staying at the center, along with six to ten students and staff from various regions in China.

With this routine, I became healthier and stronger than I had been in my entire life. In addition to the consistent physical exercise and meditation, the diet provided me with optimal nutrition. We ate fresh, whole foods, which I found delicious. As my body and mind were transforming and I was being further removed from the daily obligations of my life back home, I was learning to let go and enjoy whatever I was experiencing in the moment. An example of this occurred one morning at breakfast.

Our usual breakfast consisted of hot rice cereal (congee), steamed buns, fresh ginger, dates, nuts, pickled vegetables and a hard-boiled egg. After about a month of the same menu, I woke up one morning thinking how much I would enjoy a sprinkling of sugar on my rice cereal. As we sat down to eat breakfast after our Tai chi and Qigong practice that morning, right in front of me on the table was a small bowl of sugar. Now I had not said a word to anyone, on that day or any other day, about wanting sugar. I sprinkled it onto my rice cereal and ate silently;

with what I am sure was a very satisfied smile on my face. It was the only day there would be sugar on the table in two months' time. Whether I had somehow intuited that sugar would be offered that day, or the sugar had manifest due to my intention, or whether it was merely synchronicity, I will never know. Perhaps some things are best left a mystery, so we can simply enjoy wondering about them. I do know that each time I recall this event it brings a smile to my face.

During my time in China I learned numerous lessons that have served me well on my road toward peace. A number of those lessons, however, were learned not while I was at peace, but in the midst of frustration and anger, both my own and from those around me. Without going into detail, two of my fellow travelers complained incessantly, and the more they complained, the more they found something to complain about. As I observed this, I realized that the less I complained, the less I found something to complain about (which apparently gave them more to complain about). When we learn not to complain, we come to understand there really is not much to complain about. This is not to say we should remain silent when we witness or experience genuine injustice, but there is a time and place for such an expression. To complain constantly and play the perpetual victim does not serve anyone and can become an annoying habit to everyone involved. This was the situation I found myself in when I was told our group would travel to Tibet for several days.

We set off early one morning, and after a torturous 12-hour van ride from Tian Long Gong in Sichuan to what seemed like the middle of nowhere in the mountains of Tibet, we found ourselves at an elevation of about 14,000 feet on the highest plateau in the world. The roads we took seemed impassable at times and the scenery along the way was breathtaking. Conditions were far from comfortable, however. Seven of us were crammed into a Chinese van, which was about two-thirds the size of a standard American minivan. Adding to the discomfort of cramped quarters and the constant grumbling of two of my traveling companions was the fact that after many days of dampness, intense training, and rustic living conditions, two old injuries had resurfaced, and now my lower back and knee were screaming at me the whole way. As a result, I was actually grateful when, at one point along the drive, traffic stopped in both directions while a section of road was paved by hand – a situation which forced us to wait by the side of the road for almost two hours. Despite my discomfort, I enjoyed the break. I sat down in the grass and relaxed while watching nomadic horsemen riding far off in the distance against a backdrop of rolling mountains on the seemingly endless plain. The Tibetans, who were traveling this road and sharing our fate of having to wait until the paving project was complete, were quick to smile and very interested in the English words I was writing in my journal. We shared a fair amount of laughter, despite not understanding each other's language.

None of the discomforts and difficulties that arose along the way deterred me from absolutely knowing I was in the right place at the right time. Even though I had no idea where we were going, other than it was somewhere within Tibet, I knew this trip would be worth it. I also realized that the grueling nature of our travel was an integral part of the experience. As the proverb goes, "It is not the destination, but the journey."

Once traffic was moving again, we drove up out of the plains into the mountains and arrived at what

I can only describe as a trailer shack. It was the size of a mobile home, and to say it was in less-than-good condition would be an understatement. The meager furniture was old and quite worn, and there was no indoor plumbing. It was truly a picture of abject material poverty. Yet the inhabitants of this house, who included a lama (living Buddha), a young child, and several men and women, were all beautiful both inside and out, friendly, quick to smile, and welcoming.

My understanding of their circumstances was constrained by a slow and imprecise translation process, which entailed a Tibetan speaking in Tibetan to a Tibetan who was traveling with us, who then relayed the message in Mandarin and broken English to me, who had a limited vocabulary in Mandarin. From what I was able to piece together, however, the lama's temple had been either burned or destroyed, and according to governmental policies, once a temple was lost, it could not be rebuilt. Clearly these people had suffered a loss and had no choice but to live in extreme poverty, yet they gave no evidence of resentment. They fed and housed us graciously, and all I felt emanating from them was unconditional love.

The longer I was in their presence, the more I felt it. At one point the lama gave a 20-minute talk, not one word of which I understood, since I recognized only two Tibetan words (one for "thank you" and one for "friend"). By listening with my heart, however, I was able to receive his underlying message of kindness and compassion. After the talk he gave each of us a traditional silk scarf blessing. At some point later on, he looked into my eyes for literally five minutes. No words were spoken, yet I understood. It was an intensely powerful experience, after which I would never be the same. In the midst of losing everything, in the midst of living in such poverty and physical difficulty, these were the most genuinely loving and compassionate people I had met in this lifetime. They truly had no agenda and no judgment, and they received their life as a gift, regardless of outer circumstances.

My encounter with these exceptional people prompted me to become more aware of when my actions and the actions of others are motivated by a desire for some type of gain or special recognition, in order to further an imagined position in life. This awareness, along with my newfound understanding that we can be loving and happy without worldly possessions or recognition, would be tested with regularity, not only for the remainder of my time in China, but especially when I returned home to a life of family, career, and all the trappings of life in our material culture.

I had traveled to China expecting certain kinds of lessons, but along the way encountered one far beyond what I could have imagined. It came in the form of the opportunity to witness firsthand, through the example of some extraordinary Tibetans, that when material gain and recognition are no longer priorities, we can lead truly fulfilling lives, marked by deep love and compassion for all beings. The gift these people gave me was a living demonstration of what it means to follow the way of peace and speak with the voice of peace. I am forever grateful.

Chapter 6

MARY

*When we learn to receive with humility
and without shame,
we can then know what it is to give
without judgment.*
-Rich Marantz

In the year 2004 I had been a dedicated, daily practitioner of Tai chi and Qigong for 15 years. My daughter, Jade, was about one year old, and my wife, Lorrie, had stopped working to be a stay-at-home mom. To help make ends meet, in addition to teaching Tai chi, I worked part-time as a bartender in a restaurant in Vermont.

One particular day at the restaurant, as was my habit, I wiped the bar clean to begin the process of setting up to get ready for the night shift. No one else was around, as my co-workers were all in another area of the restaurant attending to their opening duties. As I continued through my set up routine, I noticed a medal on the bar that had not been there when I had wiped it down just ten minutes earlier. I picked it up and recognized it as a Christian religious medal. Since I was born into and raised in the Jewish tradition, I had no clue whose image was on the medal, so I decided to ask a waitress with whom I worked, who I knew to be a devout Catholic. I showed her the medal and asked, "Is this St. Christopher?" (He was the only saint I knew of, and I also remembered childhood friends having St. Christopher medals.) Her response was, "No, this is the Blessed Mother, Mary."

Knowing her deep devotion, I gave my co-worker the medal, but as I walked away, a feeling from within told me I should keep it. I told my friend I would like to hold onto the medal after all, and she gladly returned it to me. Not knowing what I was going to do with it, I set it down on the cash register for the evening and got to work. It was an extremely busy night: three deep at the 12-seat bar with the printer tape running constantly, asking me to make drinks for those who were sitting at tables eating dinner. Each time I would use my cash drawer during that evening, the medal would catch my attention.

About halfway through the night, at the height of the busyness, a customer at the bar looked up at me and said, "I think this guy is in trouble," indicating the man on his right, who appeared to be choking on his dinner. Drawing upon training as an emergency medical technician which I had received many years prior, I asked the man if he could talk. He waved his hand to indicate no. Without hesitation, I quickly walked around the bar, weaving my way through the crowd to get to him. Again I asked, "Can you speak?" He gave another wave of the hand to signal no. I then proceeded to apply the Heimlich maneuver, which succeeded in dislodging a piece of meat that was blocking his airway. "Are you okay now?" I asked.

This time he gave a verbal response, "Yes."

I then went back to work and to my surprise the man who had been choking just moments earlier went back to eating. When he finished his meal, he paid and left without saying a word.

During this entire event, even though I could feel myself going through the motions of helping someone in distress, it did not feel as if my actions were coming from me. It felt as if they were coming *through* me, and I was simply a conduit. I was reminded of this feeling when a year later a gentleman came into the bar who, in the course of our conversation, asked if I was working the night a man had been choking. He had witnessed the whole scene and said how amazed he was that nobody else seemed to notice what was going on. It was as if the action at the crowded restaurant bar and the drama of my intervention to help a choking man, even though they were happening simultaneously, were entirely separate in both time and space.

The night it happened, I continued to finish what was a very busy shift, the whole time knowing that Mary had entered my life and played a role in saving a man's life. Not until I was cleaning up at the end of the night did I realize I had found the medal at the seat of the customer who so matter-of-factly alerted me that the man next to him needed help. That night

I attached the medal of Mary to a silver chain and have worn it each day since.

Just one week later, another incident occurred in which I again felt Mary's presence guiding my actions. This time I was walking home from work at about 11:00 p.m., when suddenly I heard loud screaming coming from a car driving up the road behind me. Since 11:00 p.m. in a small Vermont town is generally quiet, with little to no activity, my initial thought was that some teenagers were having their idea of fun. As the car drew closer and the screaming grew louder, I turned around and saw the inside lights of the car were on and knew immediately this was not just some kids having fun. Suddenly the passenger door flew open, and the car stopped about 30 feet in front of where I was standing. The passenger, a young woman, jumped out of the car screaming. The driver, a young man, jumped out after her and ran around the car to grab her. She was kicking, screaming, and flailing her arms, as he picked her up and attempted to force her back into the car.

There was no time to think. I ran toward them, and when I approached within ten feet, I drew upon what is called tiger energy. This is a form of energy

I developed while learning the art of full contact fighting, using Tiger style from the system of Five Animal Kung-fu, and the self-cultivation practice of Tiger Qigong (energy exercises). On this particular night, I activated the energy by simultaneously stomping my front foot, thrusting both palms forward, and projecting the sound, "Hey" with the power of a tiger's roar rising from deep within my belly. With that, everything stopped. The attacker dropped his prey and looked at me, as did she. Before either one had a chance to react, I moved quickly and placed my body between them. My back was to her, as I faced him. By then she was in hysterics, her sweater half torn off, and he was yelling at me, trying to justify his actions. Instead of attempting to physically subdue him, which I had no desire to do, I gently swept my hand in a downward motion while repeating, "You know this is not the right thing to do." After a few minutes the man calmed down, got in his car, and left.

Apparently someone had called for help, because the police arrived shortly after the attacker drove away. As they proceeded to question me and the woman, the suspect (who turned out to be her boyfriend) returned. Surprisingly enough, he came back to give the woman a jacket she had left in his car. At that point, he was arrested and I walked home.

As with the choking incident the week before, the actions I took that night were not of me, but through me. Once again, I served as a conduit. At the time I had no doubt and still have no doubt, that Mary played a role in what happened that night. From then on, I knew The Blessed Mother would play a significant role in my life and would always be with me to provide guidance and comfort. Strength of faith such as this is not something that can be known from the intellect, which needs to find an explanation in order for it to make sense. It is a conviction that comes from an indisputable feeling from within that can only be understood through direct experience.

From the time of these two incidents up to this present day, I often find that Mother Mary is a focal point in my prayers. As I embrace her unending patience and unreserved love, sometimes by simply holding her in my awareness, my mind calms and my heart softens. Both in dreamtime visitations and through my sensing of her presence during waking hours, she has provided me with clarity and simple wisdom in times of uncertainty, as well as solace in times of distress. Most importantly, she is a primary source of energy that motivates my actions as I learn and share the message that the capacity for peace lies within each one of us.

Chapter 7

FAMILY

If we have no peace, it is because we have forgotten that we belong to each other.
-Mother Theresa

The year was 2005. I was driving south to the Jersey shore to see my family. I had a lot on my mind, because my father was at the end stage of his life. I had seen him and my mother only once in the past 13 years, when, as they were traveling through Vermont, we met for lunch one year earlier. As for my three older brothers, it had been decades since my last visit with them.

It had been my choice to separate from my family

all those years before. Periodically throughout those years of estrangement, when I would tell people about it, many times their reaction was that I was lucky not to have to deal with family. I felt differently, however. "It is not a choice I make lightly," I would respond, because to be without our original family is very difficult, and I would have preferred not to be in the position where I felt compelled to disengage from them. At the time, I believed in order for me to go through my process of releasing old emotional garbage and to grow as a spiritual being it was necessary to separate from my parents and siblings. In retrospect, I can see that because I was unwilling to stand up for myself and speak what I knew to be true, I allowed myself to be in a position of extreme discomfort in the years leading up to the separation.

Each time my parents would visit me in Florida, where I moved right after graduating from high school, I would spend three weeks prior to each visit feeling anxious. During their visits, as they spent time in my home, I would feel increasingly invisible and invalidated as a human being, a familiar feeling that I had brought with me into adulthood. Each time they would leave, I would spend another three weeks feeling depressed. After going through this cycle one too many times, I told myself I would not tolerate it anymore, at which point I asked my parents not to visit me in the future. As for my three older brothers, we never really had a relationship in the first place and so were already disconnected.

From my perspective, the house where I was raised held six people living six separate lives. From childhood through adolescence, I felt very much on my own, with no sense of heartfelt connection to the family I was living with. These were the very people who were supposedly helping to form my character. Within this framework of familial disconnection, the sense of alienation I experienced was painful and increasingly intolerable as I entered adulthood. I came to the realization that I had to change this pattern of not speaking my truth and of feeling I had no value as a person, or at some level I would perish. Releasing this dynamic seemed vital, actually a matter of life or death. Yet in the presence of my parents, I would feel myself drawn, almost hypnotically, into that old way of being I was working so hard to break away from. At the time when I chose to detach from them, I believed the only way I could resolve this conflict was by withdrawing completely from the two people who triggered an old and toxic response in me. It was necessary, I felt, not only for my own sense of peace, but for the peace of all involved. This was the background, then, in which I found myself at the time of my father's crossing.

By the time I made this trip, I had been through much spiritual training and practice, healed many emotional wounds, and was, to a great extent, comfortable in my own skin. It occurred to me, as I was driving towards the Jersey shore, that what I most desired from my family was acceptance for who I was, which included everything I had become since my accident. Then it hit me. How was I approaching them? Was I accepting my parents and brothers for who they were, whether they had grown or not? After all, if I wanted their full and complete acceptance, then I must be willing to reciprocate. This meant accepting them, whether or not they were able to accept me.

In that moment I decided I was going to be fully me, no mask. At the same time I was going to allow my family to be fully who they were. No change needed from anyone. We were all flawed and yet perfect at being who we are. This understanding freed me to present myself without any need to pretend to be something else and to do that without thinking it was in spite of them, or because I was better.

It was simple, I told myself. Be who you are and allow others to be who they are. Getting along with my family was a two-way street. I would remain true to myself, but at the same time, I needed to meet everyone on their own terms, without judgment or agenda. "How do I do this, when there is such a strong emotional connection and history?" I asked myself. The answer that came to me seemed so simple "Don't treat them like family; treat them like people." By the time I walked through my parents' front door, there was no agenda on my part, no need for revenge, no need for forgiveness, no need to pretend. My intention was simply to be there and join with my family at the end of my father's life.

Over the following weeks I made several trips to see my family and, in particular, my father. The night he crossed over I had the opportunity to sit by his bedside, hold his hand, and through this link, send in loving light. We spoke little, but we both agreed that what had been in the past no longer held any importance. What has been done has been done. All that mattered was happening right at that moment. We were at peace.

Through this experience I came to understand that, for each of us, a top priority in this lifetime is to be at peace with our parents. While it is not a requirement that we accomplish this during our parents' lifetime, the process is easier and more tangible when we can still speak to, see, and touch each other. If they are no longer on this earth, however, we can still arrive at a place of peace with them. How? Well, it really has nothing to do with them. What it hinges on is *our* attitude and whether we can accept them as they were – even if they did not accept us, even if they did not treat us well. This does not mean we have to like them or their actions, but it does mean we have to honor our connection to them and their importance in our lives.

Whether we have maintained contact with our parents or not, we will always be related to them. This cannot be changed. Not only do we share DNA, we are also linked on a metaphysical level. This bond is both tangible and mysterious. What we do has an effect on them, and what they do affects us, because like it or not, there is no separation. Whether we choose to acknowledge this and take action to repair our relationship is up to us.

One of the effects of healing and becoming more peaceful within ourselves is that it has an effect throughout our web of relationship. One way this shows up is that when we arrive at a point of peace with our parents, we are much less likely to carry our emotional garbage into the relationship we have developed with our children, leaving us free to be more loving and accepting of the remarkable spirits they are. It seems to me, the order of importance in our process of healing requires that we first be at peace with our parents, then our children, then our siblings and spouses. From there we can work our way outward to all of our other relationships and connections. Of course, what the central people in our lives do with the opportunity to heal, and be at peace through us is entirely up to them; no judgment.

As I was going through this process with my parents (my father, in particular, as he was dying) I was also going through the process with my siblings. When I set off to visit my brothers for the first time in many years, I felt myself carrying all the weight of long-held resentment, self-deprecation, and even a desire for revenge. I reminded myself, however, that I was no longer the child who was not acknowledged as a human being, and that, really, the best revenge is to be living a good life. The way to overcome resentment was to accept things as they are and not fall victim to the past. This was the mindset that framed my interactions with my family over the coming weeks, and it strengthened me – not in the sense of overcoming another, but in terms of overcoming my own demons.

The day after my father's death, I drove home to Vermont and moved from one apartment to another. Emotionally this proved to be quite difficult, as there was no time to deal with all that had occurred. I wanted to be processing my father's passing yet I was obligated to take care of my wife and daughter. It took a good six months to work through my insights and reactions to all that had happened. When I emerged from that process, it was with the knowledge and conviction that unless we achieve peace with our parents and family, we will surely block ourselves from true healing and transformation.

Chapter 8

THE CARTHUSIANS

Speaking truth is peace in action
-Rich Marantz

In 2006, while I was attending a course in traditional Chinese healing in Sarasota, Florida, my wife phoned to tell me that a monk from the Carthusian Monastery, located near our home in Vermont, had left a voice mail message asking that I call him back.

All I knew of the monastery at that time was that the monks were cloistered, lived in silence, and did not permit uninvited visitors from the outside. I knew they had both a gift shop at the bottom of the mountain and a skyline toll road that were open to the public. This toll road, by the way, is not for the faint of heart, or for any vehicle with worn brakes. It is very steep, with switchbacks which take you to the top of Equinox Mountain, where, on a clear day, you can see a beautiful panorama of the surrounding mountains and valleys. Halfway up the mountain, the monastery comes into view, but as I mentioned, it is off-limits to the public.

I was wondering, among other things, what the monks wanted with me and how they had found me. Upon returning home, I immediately contacted the monk who had called. After a short conversation, he asked if I would come to the monastery to be of some assistance. To honor the rules of their order, I will not discuss the nature of my work with them, nor disclose their names, as they specifically asked me not to mention them. They have, however, given me permission to share my personal experience with them, as well as the lessons I learned.

On the appointed day, I drove up the steep mountain road to the Carthusian monastery, not really knowing what lay ahead. After a few miles, I pulled off the main toll road and punched in the code to open a gate which led down a side road to the monastery. As I was driving along this dirt and gravel mountain road, with nothing but forest around me, I had an overwhelming sense that I was leaving the world behind. It was a surreal experience, and I found myself praying to Mary for clarity and help in remaining open to whatever would unfold.

I came around a bend in the road and approached the grounds of the monastery, and the first thing I saw was an imposing wooden cross, which stood about 20 feet high, and a concrete wall with a very large wooden gate that was open. I drove in even though there were no signs directing me where to go. Once inside the gate, there were still no signs; nor any evidence of people, just a few bare concrete and wood buildings. I had to choose whether to turn left or right. To the right turned out to be the wrong choice. Backtracking, I went to the left and proceeded until I entered an empty courtyard. There were still no people or signs, nothing but stillness and me. My car and I felt very out of place. I got out of the car and waited.

Soon a sliding wooden door opened, revealing a monk, who was wearing a horsehair robe. He greeted me with a beaming smile and after apologizing for having kept me waiting, escorted me into a building which was cold and austere. We hurriedly walked down a hallway and entered a room where the furnishings, though modest, were neat and well-maintained, with only a few religious icons serving as decorations. It reminded me of a grandmother's living room. Apparently this was the common room in which the monks gather once a week to talk with one another. The rest of the week they spend in silent prayer.

Within a few minutes, two other monks entered with something for us to eat and drink. Since I had known before going there that everyone in that order has taken a vow of silence, I could not help but wonder how we would communicate. As it turned out, the monk who initially greeted me continued to speak openly and freely with me throughout my visit.

I was still wondering why I was here, sitting in this monastery on top of a mountain with three cloistered monks. At the same time, it felt right, and I just knew I was exactly where I was meant to be at that moment. After asking some questions about my background and training, they explained why they wanted to see me. Following that conversation, we went on to speak of prayer, of practice and discipline, of spirituality, and of the difference between living in the world and living apart from the world.

What struck me very soon into the conversation was that everything these monks spoke was truth, that is, their words had a feeling of pure intention and seemed to flow directly from their hearts. This was the first of many lessons I would learn from the Carthusians: When you speak, let it be from your heart, and speak only truth. For these monks, this was a natural extension of a life of silence and prayer, whereas for most of us in the world it often takes quite a bit of effort to speak truthfully, although the result is worthwhile. I know I am always happier and more peaceful when I make the effort. At the same time, I have observed that when I am at peace, it takes practically no effort at all to speak my truth.

Where we place our focus is what makes the difference in whether we will speak in this manner or not. In the case of the Carthusians, whose only goal and need in life is to be close to God, it seems natural to bring all aspects of their lives into alignment with truth. In contrast, if our primary focus is on fulfilling the needs, agendas, and particular outcomes we assume will improve our worldly lives, then our ability to speak directly and openly is compromised. Only when we recognize that the peace which comes from speaking truth, is much deeper than the temporary satisfaction that comes from getting what we think we want by suppressing the truth, will we be more willing to be authentic in the way we present and express ourselves.

About halfway through this meeting, a bell tolled. Excusing themselves, the monks knelt in front of an altar and prayed. This was done in the most natural and matter-of-fact manner, without any hint of show. We then resumed our conversation. At some point, I felt compelled to ask if I could share with them my experiences with Mary. They agreed and listened intently, as I related the story of helping the man who was choking and, a week later, coming to the aid of a woman who was being attacked. When I finished, they sat wide-eyed and silent, looking at one another. Had I said something inappropriate, I wondered. After some time, the head monk looked at me and said very seriously, "It is no mistake you are here." He then asked if I knew Mary was their patron. I did not.

That statement, "It is no mistake you are here," struck me as profound, and I have referred to it many times since. Although we may not know the reason something is occurring in our lives, or why we are where we are, we can take comfort in saying, "It is no mistake I am here."

After that first visit with the Carthusians, which lasted about four hours, I left the monastery with a deeper sense of peace than I had experienced up to that point in my life. Something within me had transformed, moving me beyond the framework of my previous understanding. I was given a glimpse of what it means to be truly at peace, even though I had no way to reference what it was I was feeling. "What do I do with this sensation and experience?" I asked myself. I had no idea, but it was clear that my focus in life would be to find a way to live in a state of peace.

Not only did I come away from that first meeting with the Carthusians wanting to experience true peace on a sustained basis, I also came away asking,

"How is the secluded life of these monks helpful to the world?" They have left behind worldly pursuits, maintain practically no contact with society, and devote their day to prayer, with minimal time allotted to taking care of their daily necessities. How does that serve humanity?

I have a number of friends and colleagues who believe that the difficulties of daily life in our culture are such a distraction from maintaining a spiritual practice that they wish for the life of a cloistered monk. At first glance, such a life may appear easier than facing up to the difficulties associated with working at a job, family, taking care of a household, and finding time for a daily practice. However, while life in a monastery is no doubt simpler in many respects than living in society, it most certainly is not easy.

The life of a Carthusian monk involves complete and undistracted devotion to prayer and God, requiring one to leave behind all aspects of life in society prior to entering the order. Very few people have the psychological make-up and unwavering fidelity to endure the inevitable trials and tribulations such a solitary and silent way of life brings with it.

Perhaps this is why, as one Carthusian told me, "You do not enter into this way of life unless you have been called by God."

For the most part, our spiritual practice is wherever we are and if we spend our time feeling it is elsewhere, then we are sure to be disappointed when we get to where we believe "there" is. The reality of our lives is that there really is no "there." That is a fantasy, a dream, an illusion. All that exists for us to work with is this moment in time. I, for one, feel that dealing with the reality of living in the here and now keeps me plenty busy, without having to chase a fantasy of out "there".

Of course, it is also possible that we will hear with our true inner voice a calling to pursue a different situation, endeavor or even be led to a specific location, in the process of fulfilling our particular purpose. Clearly this was the case with the Carthusians I have encountered. When I left the mountain after this visit, it was with great admiration and respect for the dedication, devotion, and courage these monks display in following their calling and fulfilling their true purpose in life. Still, I pondered whether their life of seclusion could be helpful to the outside world.

It was not until after my second visit with them, when once again I left feeling at peace, that I found my answer. It came to me one day, as I was gazing up at their mountain, intensely aware of a meaningful heartfelt connection with the monks. I realized that as these profoundly religious men devote their time and focus to prayer, without distraction, it brings them to a very high frequency level, or vibration of energy. In other words, their practice of devotion to God purifies and raises their consciousness to such an extent that it creates a vibrant and positive energy field which others experience as uplifting. This is readily apparent when meeting the monks, who exude a feeling of vibrant health and happiness and this vibrancy extends beyond each individual monk to their environment as a whole. This is palpable when one spends any amount of time in the serenity which pervades the monastery grounds.

My understanding, then, is that the refined frequency and energy fields of the monks serve as a magnet to pull up the energy frequency for the rest of us. Like is being drawn to like, so that if we are on a path of spiritual development, the frequency we are on will be given a boost, figuratively speaking, by the frequency being emitted by these holy men. (Of course the Carthusians, though unique, are certainly not the only ones whose focus on the divine benefits all of humanity. I speak of them only because I have personally experienced the power of their devotion.) We are in need of such men and women to help raise our personal, as well as our planetary frequency and consciousness. In some ways we walk our spiritual path alone, but in other ways we all share this world of duality together, so it is imperative that we help one another along the way. As we do so, the collective spirit of the human species is uplifted.

Among other things the Carthusians demonstrate that service of this nature does not need to be direct or publicized. They go about their work silently, both figuratively and literally, without the rest of us knowing it is happening or that we are benefitting from their practice. The monks take no credit and have no need or desire to be recognized for their selfless efforts on behalf of all society. In Taoist terminology, this is the purist definition of a good deed. The Carthusians themselves have an adage, "To make saints, not to publicize them."

In the end, my question of how the secluded life and work of the Carthusain monks might benefit humanity brought me to an understanding that the most powerful help I or anyone else can give the world is to raise our own consciousness. The truth is that at any given moment of our spiritual walk, the majority of us are both giving and receiving an energy that assists all of humanity to ultimately lift itself to a frequency of peace.

Chapter 9

AWAKENING

When we see the beauty of heaven and earth,
we are moved.
When we see the beauty within our selves,
heaven and earth are moved.
-Chen, Zhi Ming

I had decided to attend a week-long Taoist meditation retreat with my teacher Master Yun Xiang Tseng (Chen) and 17 other students in the fall of 2006, at a picturesque mountain lodge in Colorado.

A child prodigy, Master Chen was chosen at the age of six by his master, Li Cheng Yu, to be raised on Wudang Mountain, China, where he was trained in the ancient arts of Tai chi, Qigong, meditation, and healing. A 25th generation Wudang Longmen (Dragon gate) Taoist priest and a true son of the Tao, Master Chen has a gift for making authentic Taoist teachings understandable. His rapport with his students reflects a strong belief that only if he maintains an open and sharing affection for them, can he impart the message of peace and hope that he has come to North America to deliver. In 1990, he immigrated to the United States, on a mission to build the first Wudang Taoist monastery in the West.

My first encounter with Master Chen was in 2003. I had been practicing Tai chi, Qigong, and other martial arts without a teacher for almost two years, when I came across an announcement for a workshop he was teaching in Atlanta. I called to inquire about him and spoke at length with one of his students. I was attempting to get a sense of Master Chen's integrity and motivations. I had discontinued studying with my previous teacher over an issue of integrity. The student I spoke with gave me Master Chen's phone number and suggested I speak with him directly. I made the call, and after a short conversation, invited him to teach a workshop in Vermont. He accepted my invitation and came a few months later to share his knowledge. I knew, following that first conversation, that I had found my teacher.

Prior to studying with him, I had numerous teachers who were generous and open in sharing their knowledge. I now believe my studies with each of them, was to prepare me to absorb the wisdom Master Chen would impart on me. In a short formal ceremony in 2006, I became a formal disciple of his and was given the Taoist name Chong Teng, (which translates roughly as "dragon leaping to the sky"), along with the lineage designation of 26th generation of the Wudang Longmen branch of Taoism.

Retreats with Master Chen are like no other. He has a way of pushing you at least 25% beyond what you imagine you can handle, and the days are filled, literally, with 18 hours of training. Given the amount of information absorbed on a daily basis, the meditations, exercises, and all the honest introspection, these retreats are an intense experience, to say the least.

I was 44 years old at the time of this retreat. For the

past several years, I had been traveling often to train and study, which placed quite a burden on my wife and young daughter. It was a strain because during those trips I was not there to physically to play my role of husband and father as well as it adding to our financial difficulties. This created great stress in my household, reflected in the fact that each time I left on one of these trips, my daughter would become ill. Although I knew I had no choice but to further my studies, I experienced a strong inner conflict and was torn each and every time I would leave. On the one hand, I was excited to have the opportunity to train and study, because I knew I would be progressing in my chosen vocation and avocation, but on the other hand, I felt guilty, because my leaving placed a strain on marriage and family. It was in the context of this life circumstance that I dove headfirst into what was to be a profoundly life-altering experience.

A few days into the retreat, I began to experience a feeling of heaviness that had been hidden within me. In retrospect, the feeling was similar to what I had described to a therapist years earlier, when I went to her in search of help to heal from my experience of childhood abuse. Although by the time of the retreat, I had been practicing Tai chi, Qigong, and related arts for 17 years, I still had a shadowy and unknown area in my deepest being, which I referred to as a "damp, dark corner of the basement."

One night during the retreat, at about 1:30 a.m., I could no longer endure this dark feeling inside me, so I got out of my bunk to look for Master Chen. Everyone else was asleep, but I found him in his room, still awake. "Excuse me, Master Chen, may I ask you a question?"

"Sure," he responded. "What is it?"

I was feeling so desperate that I decided not to hold back. "Please tell me what you see. What is it that I am holding onto?"

He looked at me and replied, "I don't see anything. I don't know what you are talking about."

"I cannot figure out what is holding me back. What is this blockage inside me?"

Master Chen could not have surprised me more with his matter-of-fact response. "Why don't

I just give you a gun, and you can shoot yourself in the head?" Not what I was expecting. "Curiosity is a bullet to your heart," he continued. "If you keep thinking that way, why don't you just shoot yourself right now and put yourself out of your misery?"

This was certainly not the response my ego wanted to hear, but it was exactly what I needed to hear to begin the process of breaking through to my inner pain. I had gone to my teacher seeking an answer to what was blocking me and left not needing to know...

Until then, one of the phrases I would often use when describing myself was, "I am just a kid from Jersey." The morning after my encounter with Master Chen, however, it hit me that Jersey is not where I am from; it is only where I began life in this body. Who I am, my original nature has been around much longer. Seen from that perspective, my life in New Jersey was simply another stop along the way, not the beginning.

In the following days of training, I was still troubled with that same feeling of heaviness that had prompted me to ask Master Chen for answers.

Apparently I was not doing a good job of hiding my distress, because on the last day of this week-long intensive, my "older brother" (as I like to refer to an older and more experienced classmate of mine) told me he wanted to speak with me privately after lunch. He sat me down in his room and asked with serious concern, "What is going on with you? What's bothering you?" I was taken aback. "Nothing, I'm fine," but we both knew I was not fine. After a few minutes of talking, out it came. "I feel so alone," I admitted, even though it made no sense. Here I was with my master and 17 colleagues, who were close friends, a wife and child, students, and friends and yet I was feeling completely alone.

Shaken and dazed, I left my friend's room and walked the short distance to where afternoon classes were to be held. As I entered the lodge, a classmate came up behind me and asked, "Rich, can we talk?"

"Sure," I replied, although I did not particularly feel like talking at that moment.

"Everyone is noticing," he said. "What is really bothering you? You need to let it out."

Oh great, I thought, here I am, feeling utterly

alone and shaken to the core, and wearing it like a neon sign on my chest. As I continued walking toward the room where my classmates and Master Chen were talking prior to class, another classmate came up next to me, put her arm around my shoulder, and said, "I love you." Now these words were not hers, and it was not the type of "I love you" I share with my wife and daughter, not even the kind of "I love you" I share with family and close friends. What I heard when she said these words was not even her voice… it was the voice of the Divine.

At that moment, everything around me became still and quiet and time seemed to stop. Divine voice was telling me, "*I love you.*" Never before had I heard these words spoken with such unconditional love. Never before had I heard the words "I love you" with the purest of energy forming them. I could not speak. I could not move.

Then it happened, I began to cry. This was out of character for me, for I have never been prone to crying, and certainly not in front of others. As a matter of fact, through the many years of processing my childhood abuse, when I knew crying would be helpful, I was still unable to let go. So here I was, with my friend's arm around my shoulder, crying and thinking it was because I was feeling so alone. The crying intensified and my body began to sway and rock. My friend neither encouraged nor discouraged the movements. She simply held a safe space for me, for which I will always be grateful.

We walked towards the living room and ended up by the French doors leading to an outside deck, where there is a majestic view of a 14,000-foot mountain peak. At some point my friend stepped away, although I was unaware of it. My crying continued to increase in intensity and while I was aware of everyone in the room, I could do nothing but what I was doing. I am sure the others saw what I was going through, yet no one intervened. I will always be grateful for their wisdom in not interfering when suddenly my legs gave out from underneath me, and I fell to my knees, wailing as I bent down to the ground, hands covering my face. Inside, I felt myself being completely broken down. My life, as I knew it, was disappearing. The psychological and spiritual trauma was so great it manifested as extreme physical pain, beyond anything I had ever experienced. In fact, at that moment I believed I was dying a torturous death; furthermore, I felt powerless to stop whatever was happening to me.

Then, suddenly, the room turned white, as if I were in a cloud. There was no longer a room, no longer my friends and master, no sound but the sound of my own wailing. In that moment, which was timeless, all that existed was God and me. I was face to face with our Creator.

This was judgment time. As I endured what I can only describe as the pain of death, I was overcome with an incredible sense of guilt. It was not the guilt of what I had done to others, but rather the guilt of what I had done to my original spirit. It was the guilt of what I had done to the gift I had received from my Creator. "Please forgive me. Forgive me, forgive me," I kept repeating over and over in my mind, as I lay there dying. How could I have treated my original self so badly? How could I have spit on it and cursed it? "Oh, please forgive me."

This went on for some time, until I had nothing left in me. Feeling totally drained of all energy, I finally half-crawled, half-walked to my teacher. "Please, Master Chen, can you help me light incense?"

He did so, without saying a word.

Once the incense was burning, I bowed to our Creator and the immortals and again begged forgiveness. I then joined the others as we took our places in preparation for class to begin. But each time I thought of my guilt, I would once again begin to cry. When this had gone on for about an hour, I asked, "Master Chen, can I speak it?" With his permission, I went on to explain to the group what was happening to me. While sharing my experience, I realized I was not really asking God's forgiveness. What I was asking for, and what I needed, was to forgive myself.

Master Chen teaches that, "If you don't learn to forgive, your life will always be off track." Ironically, on the first day of the retreat, I had written a brief poem, titled *Forgiven*, which went like this:

Why hold onto what has been?

*I will no longer continue to maintain the wall
between me and Tao;*

*When I erase what is written on the board,
there is nothing left to forgive.*

*Can I allow wisdom to arise and
realize it is so simple?*

The major lesson of my awakening can be
summed up very simply. From that moment forward,
I knew there is nothing I can gain in life that is worth
diminishing my spirit. I have been through many
painful experiences of a physical, emotional, or
mental nature in my life. I would rather relive all that
pain than to once again feel the spiritual pain I felt the
day of my awakening. Why? Because the difference
between the pain of mind or body and the pain of
spirit is like the difference between a firecracker
and a large bomb. I had just experienced the bomb
– a pain of spirit that was self-inflicted and had
accumulated over a lifetime of ignoring and covering
over spirit. I learned later, however, that what waited
on the other side of that pain was a spiritual energy
of immense and powerful love. So from this point
forward, I vowed my priority would be to nourish
my spirit, regardless of any consequences to my ego-
driven mind. On this point my intention was strong
and clear. The next step, then, was to follow through
with that intention in the context of everyday life.

I was now looking at the world in a totally new way. Some might call it being reborn, but as I have indicated, I thought of it as waking up or *awakening*. I could no longer claim to be unaware of what I was doing to myself. I could no longer say, "I cannot help it," because now I could help it. I was awake and no longer unconsciously living an egotistical need-driven life. Furthermore, I was ready to accept the responsibility that comes with focusing on spirit. That responsibility, as Master Chen puts it, is to "Stop pointing the finger outward; begin by pointing at yourself." I could no longer hold others accountable for my life, only myself.

How could I begin the process of developing, applying, and embodying this information? That is the question I posed to myself, as I returned to my life of chosen obligation with wife, child, job, home, and a daily physical and spiritual practice. Eventually I decided that the place to begin was with the foundation of virtue, which is the application of Tao.

The Merriam-Webster dictionary defines *virtue* as "conformity to a standard of right, a particular moral excellence, a beneficial quality or power of a thing, manly strength or courage, a commendable quality or trait, and a capacity to act." The virtue I am speaking of, however, encompasses all these definitions and more. It includes the idea that within each one of us, there is a voice – a true voice, a voice that will never lie to us, and a voice that will never lead us down the wrong path. In the art of self-defense, we call this voice our inner bodyguard. It is the voice of our original spirit, which is intimately connected to the all-encompassing spirit. In fact, there is no separation. When we learn not only to listen to and let this inner voice guide us, but also to have the courage and strength to act upon that guidance, we can honestly say we are, at that moment, living a virtuous life.

In my case, there was a wonderful and unexpected result that arose from my awakening and consequent shift in focus. As I mentioned before, just prior to my direct experience with our Creator, I had been consumed with the idea and feeling of being all alone in this world. What I came to understand is that when we disconnect from our original spirit by placing emphasis on the needs of the ego, or what is called *shi shen* (intellectual spirit in Taoist terminology), we will always be alone, because we will have separated ourselves from the essence of all life. However, when we connect to and listen to our original spirit, *yuan shen*, we maintain our connection to God and through God, to all life.

Since my awakening experience, I have never again felt alone, not once. This does not mean I do not, at times, want the company of others, I do. This also does not mean I am at all times living an upright and virtuous life, I am not. What I can confidently say, however, is that since this experience, I have made a sincere effort to live what I call a virtuous life and remain focused on that as my top priority.

Perhaps for the first time, I began living a life based on principle first and details second. This means that the voice of spirit takes precedence over the voice of ego. If the circumstances (details) of my life do not work out the way I believe I want them to, I am able to maintain a clear conscience, so long as I feel I am being true to my spirit. I do not beat up on myself or blame others, which is the way of ego. On the other hand, when life works out just as I would have hoped, I do not take credit for it, which is also the way of ego.

I find that when I am living a virtuous life, one that is open and connected to my original spirit, I truly know that everything which happens in my life is a gift from Spirit. At the same time, I also acknowledge that, without me, none of it would happen. So what does this tell me? It tells me that in everything I do, I am in partnership with Spirit. I do not try to play Spirit's role in my life, but rather set my intention to open up and allow an endless divine energy and wisdom to come through and fill me, at which point I follow to the best of my ability. It is due to this understanding that I know I am never alone. I, we are connected to Tao and through Tao.

This understanding has allowed me to accept my life for the gift that it is. When I was beginning my journey and the details of my life did not go my way, I would say, "This sucks. My life sucks. I want out!" As I continued on with my journey and diligently practiced Tai chi, Qigong, meditation and applied the related life philosophies, and the details of my life did not go as I wished, I would say, "This is so difficult. Why is life always so hard? I always have to work so hard." As I continue with my journey and practice, when life comes at me, I say, "Okay, this is a crisis. How can I see the opportunity? How can I see the silver lining?" I then reached a point where I say, "How interesting" when challenging situations arose. Then came my awakening, and I find myself saying, "Yes, this is happening and life is so great; I feel I must pinch myself, because I think I am dreaming."

For the next three years, I continued to develop my foundation, doing my absolute best to live with virtue and principle which paved the way for my second awakening.

Chapter 10
KNOW YOURSELF

Respect the mud, enjoy the flower
-Yun, Xiang Tseng (Chen)

My first awakening was the culmination of decades of practice and occurred in a condensed amount of time with very specific experiences leading up to it. My second experience of awakening, however, followed a three year process that involved numerous seemingly unrelated events which took place in the midst of living an everyday life. Many of these events unfolded both while I was diligently engaged in my daily Tai chi, Qigong, and meditation practice, and while I was participating mindfully in the mundane situations that make up the ordinary life of a husband and father.

I came home from that retreat in Colorado knowing with certainty that my priority was to nourish my spirit, regardless of the consequences to my ego-driven mind. This was quickly tested and with regularity. My marriage was troubled and strained to the breaking point, my daughter was having ongoing health issues, I was in a state of perpetual financial crisis, my 150 year-old house was in constant need of attention, and I was working many hours teaching Tai chi and bartending, trying to keep it all afloat. In short, life was happening, whether I was awake or not. Although I had a strong formal daily discipline of practice, the ordinary moments and challenges of my ongoing life became the true crucible in which I would practice and apply all that I had learned.

Over time my perception of life had altered dramatically, due in large measure to years of receiving and integrating the teachings of practical Taoist philosophy. Central to these teachings and my transformation was an understanding of, and detachment from, the games of ego. For one thing, I recognized that a tactic ego uses to control us is to persuade us that what we have is not enough, be it money, status, relationships, or something else, and that we need *more*. Ego then devises a succession of schemes in which we attempt to get what we have come to believe we need. When we do fulfill those needs, we might experience a temporary satisfaction or brief happiness, but it doesn't last. That is because an altogether different perspective is required to anchor an ongoing state of happiness that is not dependent on outer circumstances. There is a Taoist saying: *When we know enough is enough, we will always be happy.*

Another major tactic of ego is what Master Chen refers to as the "triangle game." This refers to our tendency, at any given moment in time, to play the part of victim, persecutor, or hero. We regularly take on these roles at a subconscious level, and the tool our mind uses to keep us in the game is judgment – of self, as well as others. We will continue this charade until we begin to be aware that we are caught in the game. Only by paying attention and being honest with ourselves can we catch sight of ourselves playing the triangle game with various partners in our life.

The perfect opportunity for me to practice

awareness of this ego game presented itself in the strained relationship between my wife and me, which had reached the point where heated arguments were a common occurrence. Once I started to apply my understanding of how the ego operates to this central relationship in my life, I could see clearly how entrenched *both* of us were in the game of acting out the roles of victim, persecutor, or hero. Viewing our interactions from this perspective, I was better able to step back and detach from the game, letting go of judgment and any particular outcome I thought I wanted. Each time I did so, the wall of negativity between my wife and me would noticeably soften – that is, until we replayed the dynamic again, at which point I would have to once again become aware of the triangle game we were playing and detach yet again.

As this cycle repeated itself many times, one of the hardest things I grappled with was to resist judgmental comebacks like, "Why are you being such a victim?" or "Why are you attacking and judging me?" However, I persisted in returning over and over again to my practice of not pointing the finger outward in blame and of releasing judgment, both of myself and my wife. This created an opening for me to move toward accepting each of us as we are which, in turn, allowed the wall between us to dissolve. Eventually we found common ground, where we live together as a family in awareness.

A question we may ask ourselves is how can we detach from ego games yet still be active members of society? The answer I would give goes back to what my practice has focused on since awakening in Colorado: cultivating virtue, the practice of listening to our true voice and having the courage and strength to act upon the wisdom from within. This will lead us to what is called the three treasures of Tao: conscience, mercy, and compassion.

When we are living with virtue, we can sleep at night knowing that even if things did not work out the way we thought we wanted, we could not have acted in any other way and still have nourished our original spirit. We are at peace knowing we have nourished our spirit above ego. This can be called *conscience*. When our conscience is clear, our spirit is nourished and rises. When our spirit rises, our perspective is objective, and we see a situation for what it is. At that point we become aware of our role within the game that is being played.

We recognize that everyone involved in the situation is simply being human and in any given moment, either feeding ego or nourishing spirit. This recognition of the humanity within ourselves and others might be called *mercy*. When we are being merciful by recognizing the humanity within us all, we see that everyone is doing the best they can at that moment. We see that no one really does anything *to* us; rather each one of us is involved in playing a role within the human experience we all share together. From this vantage point, we become aware that we are all one, and when we truly grasp this, we can act with compassion for self, as well as others. When we view humanity with *compassion*, we can forgive – although there is no longer a need to forgive, because there is no longer judgment.

Nurturing these three treasures of Tao – conscience, mercy, and compassion – will take us to a place where we can release judgment of self and others. This, in turn, empowers us to detach from the games of ego, which, frees us to reenter a worldly arena without being played by the game, because we no longer have a need to play. As Master Chen teaches, "We can play with life, or life can play with us." When we release attachments to this ego-based life we are free to live a fully genuine and loving life within this world of illusion and to thoroughly enjoy that life, regardless of whether the situations we find ourselves in appear on the surface to be pleasant or unpleasant.

Following my awakening in Colorado, I continued to apply these spiritual principles not only in the relationship with my wife, but also with everyone I encountered. In the process I learned something incredibly important. When we ask ourselves what it is that we want, the only truly satisfying answer is, "To be at peace." Any other answer involves the transient and changeable details that make up our daily lives and bring only short-term conditional happiness. However, when we approach our life knowing that what we want from any given situation is to be at peace, this provides a foundation for most situations to evolve peacefully, without struggle.

Dancing when the rooster crows
to follow the Taoist passion,
With three treasures in hand,
the goal is here and now.
This lonely path is straight and narrow.....
Seven stars on a cloudless night
reveal the true purpose,
Connected to Tao we are never alone.
-Rich Marantz

After those three years of diligent practice, I reached another turning point in my life. It was ushered in with a nocturnal visit, which set things in motion for me to awaken once again.

She came in a dream, just before dawn one morning in 2009. There was no face and no body, yet I knew who it was. Mary's presence was unmistakable and her voice clear. *"Share my message of peace. This is a message of peace. Teach others the way of peace."* That was it – brief, but powerful. I awoke with a strong sense that I had been called to act, called to share, and teach the message of peace.

What was unsaid, but understood within the

dream, was that I would be guided as to when it was time for me to act. Well, the time came quickly – that morning, in fact. I was teaching my weekly modified Tai chi class for a group of 13 elderly people, average age 85 to 95, many in wheelchairs or using walkers. We were proceeding through a series of sitting movements, when I heard Mary's voice as clearly as if she were standing behind me. *"Now is the time; teach my message of peace."*

" What? Now? But you didn't tell me how. How do I teach this?" It was a very real appeal. I did not feel qualified. I did not feel worthy, wise, or experienced enough to teach what I was being asked to teach.

Her answer came quickly, yet so patiently, as if speaking to a child. *"You don't have to do anything. Just be who you are. Simply be yourself."*

"Really, that's it? Well, I can do that." I thought. In Mary's wisdom, she knew that if I were to accept my calling, I could do it in this situation, where I need do nothing other than be myself. This group of elderly students, whom I had been teaching for several years, was already completely accepting of who I was and showed me unconditional love. It was a perfect place to begin. So on that day and in that room, I began the process of answering Spirit's call to purposely teach a simple message of peace. I set my intention to be who I am while sharing this knowledge, to teach from my heart, and to remain open to listening to the voice of Spirit while speaking.

Not long after receiving Mary's request, I took my second trip to teach a Tai chi workshop in Austin, Texas. During that trip, which was noteworthy on every level, I found I was being more myself than at any other time in my life. As I interacted with the people I was to meet and teach, each remarkable in his or her own way, I would for the first time in my life not feel that I either needed to be, or not be, like any other person. Several years of practice had culminated in my leaving behind enough of my ego-based way of being that I was able to spend the weekend in a state of full acceptance. Not only was I appreciating these dedicated and exceptional people for who they were, I looked upon myself with appreciation as well. I was not trying to be anyone else. I was simply being me, flaws and imperfections included, and I felt thoroughly comfortable in my own skin.

During my time in Austin and the week following my return home, I was receiving small insight after small insight. It hit me that I was on the threshold of a second awakening, and how very different it was from the first. In 2006, I had suffered the pain of a dying ego and could not stop crying. Now, three years later, I was experiencing the genuine joy of being alive. I was seeing through the illusion of this ego-driven world and I fell instantly and deeply in love with it. For the first time I understood beyond a theoretical level something Master Chen had said many times over the years, "Respect the mud, enjoy the flower."

This was his way of referring to the lesson of the lotus flower. This beautiful flower, which represents our original spirit, grows out of the mud. The reflection for us is that we cannot expect our flower (spirit) to blossom if we spend our time trying to get away from the mud, which represents the physical world. Even though the mud is impure, it is perfect and complete as it is and offering the ideal medium for doing what it is meant to do. So when we see clearly that the physical world is not something just to tolerate or even despise, we can appreciate it as integral for the blossoming of our spirit. At this point, we not only respect the world, we actually fall in love with it.

This all came to a head as I was driving in my car on my way to teach a class. From seemingly out of nowhere, a torrent of energy began coursing through my body, until I felt I would burst at the seams. It seemed that all the energy available to our human form was coming into and through me, and with it came a sudden realization of how ridiculous this world is. In a flash, I saw the absurdity of the importance we place on minor details of life and the insignificance of chasing after what our egos tell us we want. It all struck me as hilarious and I burst out laughing.

I parked my car, still laughing out loud, though in a state of unusual clarity. I flashed back to the first time I met Master Chen in 2003, when he gave the following teaching: "Ask me what is Tao, and I will ask you what is need?" In subsequent years, from time to time he would repeat this and speak often of need, so it was clear that I would have to understand need in order to understand Tao. Furthermore, I would have to grasp the meaning of need for myself, because Master Chen, in the tradition of true Taoist masters, was not inclined to explain his often cryptic teachings. No, that would be left to the student, whose understanding would generally emerge in layers over time. What I understood was that when Master Chen spoke of need, he was not referring to our basic need for food, clothing, and shelter, but rather to a deep and hidden need that feeds ego and blocks us from Tao. But what that need was exactly, I could not say.

As I sat in my parked car that day, six years after Master Chen first shared his teaching to me about Tao and need, a knowing from well beyond my intellect flashed throughout my being of what the primary need is that blocks us from Tao. It is the need to set up and maintain our lives in such a way that we will cover up and forget who we really are. It is the need to obscure the magnificence of our original spirit. Again, a vast knowledge filled me with lightning-like speed. We do this because the personality-ego fears, more than anything else, that we will actually glimpse our original divine self and realize we are not separate from Tao, from God, or from the Divine. This qualifies as ego's deepest darkest fear, because should such awareness strike, it would be game over for the ego.

This awakening, a lifetime in the making, unfolded in an instant. With spiritual sight that goes way beyond mental understanding, I grasped that life in this world, which I had previously considered to be "real," was actually an illusion. Simultaneously, I *felt* throughout my being that my original self is one with Tao. In that moment my ego, or intellectual mind (my *shi shen*), which was having a grand time creating and maintaining this illusion I called my life, went from master to servant in the blink of an eye.

In that moment and in each moment since, I have recognized that although I am living the life of a guy named Rich, that is not who I am. Like the lotus flower which thrives in the mud, I will respect and love this physical body and this guy named Rich so that the original spirit that I am, which cannot be seen or described and is intimately connected to Tao and God, can grow and blossom.

Chapter 11

MESSENGERS OF PEACE

What do you have that you have not received,
and if you have received it,
how can you boast about it?
-Corinthians 4:7

None of us are alone on our path. Loving support and guidance is always available, and it is my belief that each and every one of us has the ability to hear exactly what it is we need to hear, precisely when we need to hear it.

I have already shared with you some vivid instances of guidance I received at pivotal moments on my journey: the time Divine voice guided me out of the ocean when I was at risk of drowning at age 12, the time my friend uttered the words "I love you" as I was on the edge of a transformative awakening experience, and the time Mother Mary visited me in a dream to ask that I teach her message of peace. Most guidance, however, is received in far less dramatic fashion.

It was while attending a workshop with Master Chen in 2006 that I became aware of an intriguing truth about the nature of spiritual guidance. As I interacted with my classmates at that workshop, as well as with strangers I encountered outside class, I began to notice that either I would say something another person would need to be hearing, or another person would say something that was just right for me to hear. As I paid closer attention to this phenomenon, I observed that at any given moment, anyone can serve as a conduit for the energy of spirit and function as a messenger for another person. I believe this occurs on a regular basis, although many of us do not realize we are being given guidance through the people we meet.

This phenomenon of giving and receiving messages is happening whether we are aware of it or not, in much the same way we all experience dream during sleep. The messages of those dreams are there, regardless if we receive what they are telling us or not. To serve as a messenger, or to allow ourselves to be the recipient of a message, is a choice we can make consciously to help guide us through this muddy world. From my perspective, any help we can get or give on our way to peace within this life is certainly worth the effort.

If we remain open and receptive, we can intuit that what we are saying to another person is really coming through us from a higher level than personality-ego. Many times something will pop into my head, which I recognize as a message for a specific person, even if it is someone I have just met. I sometimes refer to the feeling I have when this happens as getting a "hit." When it occurs, the quality of thought feels different to me than the quality of thoughts originating with my intellect and emotions. Sometimes the message comes through as one word, at other times as one or more sentences. When I am aware of what is going on, I do my best not to change even one word, because I feel these words are not coming *from* me, but *through* me and changing the wording would be like delivering a letter to someone, but editing it prior to delivery.

When on the receiving end of such an exchange, I have noticed that it often occurs in the midst of ordinary conversation, in a situation where the other person is very likely unaware that their words are directly relevant to an issue or problem I am working through. The way I recognize when someone is saying something I need to hear is by tuning in not only to the meaning of their words, but also to the quality and energetic frequency with which those words are delivered. When Spirit is communicating to me through someone else, it is almost as if the words come across in **bold letters** and I get the feeling that the other person and myself have connected to help me understand what is required for my learning and healing. If I remain open and receptive, I just *know* when I am hearing a message of guidance for myself.

There is no telling when, where, or from whom, this type of message will come. I'll give an example, which occurred years before my insight that we can all serve as spiritual messengers. I had moved to Vermont from Rochester, New York, where I had been training intensively with two different teachers. One was Sifu Frederick James, who was teaching me the combative fighting art of Kung-fu, and from the other, Lin Yao, I was learning Tai chi, Qigong, meditation, and the healing arts. Once in Vermont, I set out to find my next teacher. During the search process, I visited a number of different schools and spiritual centers, one of which was a Zen Buddhist center. Although I realized quickly during a group meditation that this was not where I belonged, I nonetheless decided to stay for the lecture that followed. I did not take much notice of what was said, until the priest made this comment: *"It is good to be a seeker, but at some point you have to be a finder."* Those words made an impression. You might say they leaped out at me and in that instant, I knew who my next teacher would be.

I had already attended some of the workshops given by the Tai chi Master Jou, Tsung Hwa, and knew that I respected both his skills and integrity. However, I had not considered him as a possibility, because he was located several hours away in New York and I was assuming I would attend classes closer to home, in Vermont. That assumption shifted though, when I heard the Buddhist priest speak of becoming a *finder*. Suddenly I knew that the quality of my teacher was a more important consideration than the distance I would have to travel. From that time until Master Jou's untimely death less than two years later, I would drive seven hours round-trip every three weeks to attend his classes. Master Jou once commented to me about the distance I traveled to attend his classes. "I know I must be passing by many Tai chi teachers between my house and here," I told him, "but I know that you are serious." He simply smiled in response. It was the right choice to study with him, because he turned out to be one of my most influential teachers.

My point is that the messages and healing energies which abound in our wonderful world are not always going to show up in a spectacular way. In fact, they are very likely to show up as plain and ordinary, which requires us to pay extra attention in order to recognize their potential. There is a Zen saying: "The magic is in the mundane." An illustration of this is my interaction with rocks and the messages they can hold.

Like many people I know, I have had a lifelong love of rocks. I remember a time as a young boy, when my parents were moving me from one bedroom to another. As my father went to lift my dresser, he found it incredibly heavy. "What do you have in here, rocks?" he asked. "Yes," I answered. He opened the drawers to discover that each was filled with rocks instead of clothes, which were stuffed under the bed. This reflection of where my priorities lie has not really changed much and my connection with rocks has continued into my adulthood.

Over time I have learned to use medicine rocks to hear messages for helping others. Not long ago, I was visiting a dear friend in the hospital. She is an extremely spiritual person who lives close to the earth and nature. Somehow our conversation turned to medicine rocks, and she retrieved some rocks from a side table. As she started to hand them to me, I asked her to please give them to me one at a time. The first was a nicely carved piece of quartz. I held it in my hand, and within a few moments, I felt a vibration going up my arm. When this vibration hit my torso, I began to feel nauseous. I sat with that for a moment, until I couldn't take it anymore, "I can't hold onto this anymore," I told her. She said that she also thought the energy was not good for her and proceeded to put it away in a drawer.

She then handed me a small, round, flat white rock. I held it and again felt the vibration going up my arm. This time when the vibration hit my torso, I broke out into a smile and felt instantly happy. "The medicine of this rock is happy," I said. "Hold it whenever you think of your beloved husband." This rock, she told me, had been one her husband had kept. Next, she handed me a rock that was similar in look and feel to the one before. Again, a vibration moved up my arm, but this time when the vibration reached my torso, I was overcome with an understanding that some aspects of life are meant to be taken seriously. "This is the companion rock to the happy rock." I told her after a long pause. "They are meant to be kept together. They complement each other, happy and serious." She looked at the rocks, then up at me and said, "These two were kept together by our bed."

She then handed me a flat black rock. Nothing, no vibration, no message, just a nice looking rock; it was not a medicine rock. Lastly, she handed me a fairly large dark-colored arrowhead. I was surprised at how light it was. It must be man-made material I thought, not a rock at all. No vibration, however a message: "Take the battle with your illness lightly." She responded with a smile.

This was neither the first, nor the last time I used a particular rock to bring a message to someone else. With practice, the messages have come with greater clarity, not only in terms of knowing what a rock is to be used for, but also for whom a particular message is intended. I have come to understand that rocks carry "medicine" (a remedy for the illness of spirit) and that, for some unknown reason, they reveal their medicine to me. I realize this is not something special about me or anything I have done. I am simply a partner in receiving and sharing the wisdom of this earth. However, if I do not listen and then act on what I receive, I am not playing my role and the medicine will go unused.

With a quiet mind, patience, and practice, I believe we can begin to discern when we are being used to pass messages along to others, as well as when we are hearing messages meant for us. I view all such messages as a pure gift from Spirit and trust that if we follow their clues, they will guide us on our way to peace.

Chapter 12

FULL ENGAGEMENT

Peace is present right here and now,
in ourselves and in everything we do and see.
The question is whether or not
we are in touch with it.
-Thich Nhat Hanh

It was the summer of 2007, and I was going to be taking a car trip with my wife and daughter from our home in Vermont to the New Jersey shore to visit family. Up to this point, whenever I would go anywhere, I would plan in detail each step of the journey, incessantly going over in my mind what would happen next, looking ahead at least one or two steps beyond where I was and what I was doing.

This way of traveling, or going anywhere for that matter, had two unintended results. For one thing I would be anxious the whole time, hoping that what I had in mind would actually occur, but fearful it would not. In addition, I was not much fun as a traveling companion, because I had such a need to control what I imagined should happen next, unable to enjoy the present moment.

On this particular trip I resolved that things would be different. "But how?" I asked myself. The answer that came to me seemed so simple. "Stay present, stay in the moment." Of course I had heard this advice many times from many sources, but it still did not answer my question. How? How do I stay present and in the moment? Even with all my training, practice, and study, I had no clue how to actually do this.

As we began to prepare for our trip, a fairly basic solution occurred to me. What is in the present? Everything I see is in the present. So I would take notice of everything I could see with my eyes. What else is in the present? Everything I can hear, smell, taste, and feel with my body are in the present. So I would take notice of everything I could hear with my ears, taste with my mouth, and feel through my body. In this way I stopped myself from going outward with my mind to a future time or place beyond what any of my senses were experiencing. Instead, I allowed myself to experience the present moment through my five senses, which meant I allowed the immediate physical world surrounding me to come to me. I also did not judge what I was experiencing, nor did I let my mind wander into an interpretation and evaluation of what was happening. I simply saw, heard, tasted, smelled, and felt – alternating from one sense to another, as something new came onto the scene. In this way, I remained fully engaged in my environment.

Being fully engaged in our environment leaves no room for imagining a future fantasy environment. I say "fantasy" because what we imagine for the future is truly fantasy. Of course, we may have a preliminary and general idea of the way situations and relationships are likely to unfold, but we cannot know with certainty. When we engage with our immediate environment however, we engage in our present physical reality and the result is immediate. As we use our five senses to tune into and sample the physical world around us, our minds actually draw away from the physical and turn inward, leading us to a calm and relaxed state of being.

When I first began using this method, I needed to practice it constantly. Driving home on the New York State Thruway, for example, I would catch myself thinking about the next leg of our journey, which would trigger some anxiety. Time to engage the five senses. "What does the steering wheel feel like to my hands?" I asked myself. "What am I seeing right now? What am I hearing right now?" Sure enough, this technique rooted me in present time and had a calming effect. Before long, however, my thoughts would drift to the future and I would have to cycle through the entire routine once again. This might occur 50 times in an hour.

After engaging in and refining this process for about a month, I found myself living in the present moment for longer periods of time. I still need to use this method when life draws my focus outward, but it is comforting to know I have a practical and simple tool to bring me back into my body and back into the present moment.

This also has the benefit of increasing my energy. There is a saying in the art of Tai chi: "Where the mind goes, the *qi* goes." If the mind is anywhere other than where we are in the present moment, this puts us in a mode of leaking or dispersing energy. However, when our mind is engaged in the moment, then *qi* is contained within the body, and we are in a mode of gathering and cultivating energy.

Since the time of my family's car trip to New Jersey in the summer of 2007, I have thoroughly enjoyed each moment of each trip by using this method of focusing through my five senses to remain grounded in the present moment.

Chapter 13

KINDNESS

Peace is not merely a goal we seek,
but a means by which we arrive at that goal.
-Martin Luther King, Jr.

My wife Lorrie, my daughter Jade and I were boarding an airplane home to Vermont, following a trip to Florida. Jade who was four years old at the time, had had difficulty with flying in the past, due to extreme pain in her ears, nausea, and being overwhelmed with so many people in such a small space. We knew she would be fine, as long as we were there to comfort and help her through the experience, however, we ran into a problem as we boarded. The flight was full, there was no assigned seating, and only center seats were left. As Lorrie and I stood in the aisle with our young child, wondering what we were going to do, a woman on the aisle next to an empty center seat offered to move to the center seat in the row in front of hers. I was quite certain she did not want to travel in the center seat (who does); yet she gave up her seat with a smile and was happy to help. We thanked her and exchanged smiles.

Now Lorrie and Jade were able to sit together. I sat in the center seat across the aisle from them next to a college aged man, who had his headphones on and was engrossed in listening to his music. I was happy Lorrie and Jade were together. However, as a concerned father, I kept looking over to see how they were doing, wishing I could be closer. Even though the young man next to me did not appear to be paying attention to anyone around him, apparently he had noticed my concern, because he offered to exchange seats with me. He was quite tall, so I am sure he did not really want to be sitting in the center seat, but, like the woman, he exchanged gladly and without any apparent regret. I thanked him, we exchanged smiles, and he went back to his music. I breathed a sigh of relief.

That woman and man were acting from what Taoist philosophy teaches is the original nature of humanity: kindness. Not only were they being considerate, we (Lorrie, Jade and I) presented them with an opportunity to reveal their innate kindness. So while they were willing to put their needs aside to be kind, without wanting anything in return (which is true kindness), at the same time we extended kindness to them, by giving them a chance to express their true nature. In that moment I realized that, as humans, we feel most aligned with our nature when we are interacting out of genuine kindness. It does not matter if we are being kind to someone else, or someone else is being kind to us; all involved are sharing the experience of giving and receiving love.

I asked myself why these two fellow passengers would put aside their own comfort to help my family, while others on the plane either did not notice our plight or chose not to act? The answer, I believe, is that they felt connected to and were able to empathize with others – a characteristic of those on the road to peace.

I remember a teaching I received that was an essential component for me to walk in the direction of feeling connected to and empathetic with humanity and Tao. It was a Wednesday in the early spring of 2010, and I had practiced my Tai chi forms at home during the morning. Then, in the afternoon, I taught one private lesson and three group Tai chi classes. By the time of the last class, I had already completed many repetitions of various Tai chi movements and was feeling great. My mind was clear and calm, and a powerful energy flowed through my body. Toward the end of that class, when I was silently leading the group through a sequence of movement, I heard an inner voice, which I recognized as the voice of Spirit.

"If you took a vow of poverty, what would your life look like?" the voice asked.

"How provocative," I thought, surprised I did not resist the question right away. "What *would* my life look like if I took a vow of poverty?" I continued with class, all the while pondering this question. I did not seek an answer just then, because I knew that any answer I gave at that moment would only come from my ego, or thinking mind. In fact I knew the only way I could accurately answer the question was to take a vow of poverty, which I had no plans of doing at that time. Without taking the vow, any answer would be purely theoretical as to what would happen. I continued to hold this compelling question in my awareness, though, realizing that it called for an understanding of the values and actions which nourish my spirit, without regard for feeding ego. I knew I would be guided to an answer when I was ready to know. As I often say, "If you need to know, you will know." This was not the type of situation to be figured out. Rather, it was the type of situation that revealed itself when we allow our minds to be quiet and open.

Up to this time, my financial situation had been chronically tenuous at best. There never seemed to be enough money to meet our needs. Over the years of working as a self-employed Tai chi teacher and part-time bartender, I had to learn to be comfortable with uncertainty, never knowing how much money would be coming in on any given week. However, as the sole supporter of my wife and child – with a home, bills, and debt – this would at times cause me great distress. On many occasions, when we were faced with wondering how bills would be paid and food put on the table, my mind would be preoccupied with matters of money. I knew, of course, that many people share this dilemma, but that did not stop me from worrying, which created a serious distraction that adversely affected my spiritual practice, work, family harmony, and overall happiness. So what to do?

Over time I discovered that if I did not slip into worrying, I would be shown the route to take, and things would eventually work themselves out. When I gave into the worrying, however, I felt overwhelmed and all I would create was depression or frustration. So I began practicing the art of not worrying when I would be presented with a difficult financial situation, and with practice, I became fairly proficient.

At the same time I was trying many approaches to change our situation. I still desired things we did not have, but needed. I wrote wish lists, used visualization, worked more hours, and did without much. At some point, I realized the problem was not that I did not have enough, but rather that I had set up a life in which I needed too much. Also, I noted the connection between worrying and trusting. I saw that where there is worry, there is no trust, but where there is trust, there is no worry. So not only did I consciously stop worrying, I consciously began to practice trusting.

The practice of not worrying and trusting is less a matter of technique and more an act of remembering. It often seems that when we are patient and trust, not getting caught up in the kind of shortsighted thinking that can occur during a crisis, the situation changes in an unexpected and favorable way. It is at those times that I look back on a drama that has passed and laugh at myself for having been so anxious in the first place. So now, whenever I find myself worrying over a particular life situation, I remind myself of what I often say following a so-called crisis: "It's funny the way things work out." Of course, the key to living peacefully is to remember this *before* starting to worry. However, it is still effective even when we find ourselves already in the grip of anxiety.

Just when I thought I had all this figured out, Haa! Divine voice posed the question, "*If you took a vow of poverty, what would your life look like?*"

A few days after this question was put to me, I was having a conversation with Spirit while walking my dog. I spoke my piece and asked for guidance. The answer that came was, "*You are trusting and not worried, but why are you still concerned?*" Ouch! I was hearing the truth and it was futile to argue. Spirit was telling me that to truly trust, I must not only *not* worry, but also *not* be concerned. Upon further reflection, I realized that even when I was calm and not worried about anything in particular, I was still concerned with maintaining my life as I knew it, and with what was going to happen to me.

This brings me back to connection and empathy. As I began to learn and practice the idea of letting go of concern for self, I found that the seeming separation between me and others dissolved. When I let go of my preoccupation with, "What is going to happen to me?" I found myself, for the very first time, truly feeling the suffering and pain of others. It was not that I had been unaware of the challenges others face, but I was inadvertently receiving only a fraction of the difficulties they were undergoing, because I was so focused on my own well-being. This was a painful insight, and for several days I was quite disturbed by the harsh conditions and situations so many people encounter in their lives.

Oddly enough, as I observed this, I also began to feel an overwhelming sense of joy. I believe this was because, by stepping out of my self-absorbed concern for self, I was, for the first time, genuinely connecting with my fellow man. Not only was I feeling that connection more deeply, I was also aware of a strengthening of my connection with divinity. This was freeing. No longer was I concerned with what I would get out of the relationship with humanity or Spirit. No longer was I feeling any need beyond acceptance of what is and hope for what will be. I was simply in a state of being, without agenda. The less focus I maintained on myself, the more clearly I was able to see others and Spirit. This is something I still have to remind myself to practice, for I have yet to embody it effortlessly, as my natural way of being.

Undue concern for self, worrying, and a preoccupation with maintaining the life we have arranged for ourselves all work to blind us and lead us away from connection with our original self, our fellow man, and God. It takes discipline, dedication, and devotion to return to knowing who we have always been and to once again establish our bond with humanity and Tao.

I once heard a saying that "It takes effort to be natural." I agree, and as a result of my understanding of the need for consistent effort to develop my potential, I long ago let go of asking if something is easy or difficult. My only concern these days is whether something is worthwhile. To me, it is clear that acting from our original nature of kindness is worthwhile, that practicing the art of not worrying and trusting is worthwhile, and that letting go of preoccupation with self is worthwhile. All three practices are integral to the way of peace. Once we realize our inherent longing for peace, all effort to that end is worthwhile and when we put in the required effort, we learn that peace has been within us all along.

Chapter 14

DISCIPLINE

Never bargain with Tao.
There is no shortcut to heaven.
-Li, Cheng Yu

Everything I have spoken about thus far in this book needs to be practiced to be embodied. I truly believe there is no other way. To only know in theory what I have presented, without practical application, is like reading about hiking a beautiful mountain trail without ever putting on your hiking boots, feeling the rocks under your feet, hearing the sounds of nature, and seeing firsthand the vistas that appear after the strain of going up a steep hill. To cultivate our potential, we must put in daily effort. This is one of the common characteristics displayed by those people I have had the good fortune to meet in my life, whom I see as coming closest to reaching their potential as human beings.

As I was in the process of writing this book, I had times where my faith was being put to the test. In those moments, I found myself turning to Spirit's message of peace, and once again found that the principles do work, but they also require work. They don't do the work for you, and it is certainly not easy to hold focus and practice when you are in the thick of responding to a major challenge of one sort or another.

There are many practices we could employ to support our journey to peace. Any activity we regularly engage in that helps us unveil our true self would qualify. Some of the possibilities include physical or mental exercise, prayer, or work. In fact, I consider the writing of this book to have been a form of disciplined practice. Whatever methods are chosen, they are most beneficial when we make use of them on a daily basis and approach them with an attitude of devotion, as a means of nourishing our mind, body, and spirit. Staying power is also a consideration. When choosing a practice, I not only ask how it is likely to benefit me, but also whether I am likely to sustain it over the long term.

With respect to my own personal set of practices, I picture them fitting into a pattern of concentric circles. Which circle a practice resides in indicates how central a role it plays in keeping me healthy and moving me in the direction of fulfilling my life's purpose. The first and inner circle is reserved for core practices, which I believe offer the strongest support and nourishment for my original spirit. In my case, these include Tai chi movements (I rotate among different sequences and forms), meditation, and prayer. It is rare for a day to go by in which I do not practice all three.

Located in the circle just beyond the inner circle, are practices I use regularly, but not on a daily basis; for me these include various Qigong exercises (from vigorous Hard Qigong to gentle Primordial Qigong), Kung-fu, walks, and hikes. Circles further out are for practices I use as needed, perhaps to help with a specific health or life issue I am working through; examples of these practices would be the use of healing sounds, or a specific meditation to help me regain my equilibrium. The circles beyond that are for seasonal or occasional practices. It is important to note that I am in no way rigid about what and when I practice. I listen to my body and mind, pay attention to nature and my life situation, and then choose appropriate practices for that day.

When it comes to reaping the benefits of daily effort and discipline, there are three basic ingredients. In order of importance, they are consistency, quality, and quantity.

To understand the role they play in a long-term practice, imagine yourself setting out to make vegetable soup. You cut up a variety of vegetables and add them to a pot with broth and seasonings, which you then put on the stove to cook. What would happen if, as soon as everything started to heat up, you turned the burner off, then turned it on, and then off again? How would your vegetables, broth, and spices ever transform into soup? You get the picture. In the same way, we must get the heat turned up in our practice and then maintain a consistent simmering heat, in order for transformation to occur.

A second consideration for an enjoyable vegetable soup is the quality of ingredients. If we use vegetables that are no longer fresh or that contain toxins from chemical sprays, then even with a good amount of steady heat, which will give us a well-cooked soup, the end result will neither be tasty, nor give us the nourishment we are looking for. So our practice needs to be not only steady, but also approached with a quality of mindfulness and performed to the best of our ability.

Of final concern is quantity. If our soup is cooked well with high-quality ingredients, then we do not need a lot to nourish us, even though we may want more because it tastes so good. On the other hand, if we have a poorly cooked soup with inferior ingredients, we are not likely to feel satisfied no matter how much we consume.

The same overall formula holds true for our practice. Engage in a chosen discipline on a consistent basis, and perform it to the best of your ability, spending sufficient time each day to turn up the heat, and you will most certainly reap the benefits of nourishing your mind, body, and spirit. You may want to ask yourself whether you are doing this, or are ready to do this, with whatever practices you have chosen.

Longevity of a disciplined practice results in both short and long-term benefits. In the short-term, the majority of us experience dips and peaks in our sense of well-being. If we are at a low point on a given day, focusing on our practice might serve to balance us emotionally and lift our spirits. If, on the other hand, we are already feeling peaceful and happy, there is a possibility that when we engage in our practice, we will enter an even deeper state of connection; we may even achieve a vantage point we have never before experienced. This is what I consider a breakthrough - gifting us with the opportunity to see beyond what we previously thought was possible. Generally, I have found breakthroughs to be short-term phenomena. However, if we maintain a consistent and high-quality effort with respect to our daily focus and practice, it is likely that today's high point will eventually become tomorrow's low point. I often tell students and friends that, "Ten years ago, I could not have imagined on my best day that a person could feel as good physically, emotionally, mentally, and spiritually as I do now on my worst day." That is the long-term benefit of a disciplined practice.

To further illustrate the importance of discipline, I will relate a conversation with Master Chen, which took place at a Tai chi intensive in Texas. During one his lectures, when he was telling us about what it was like during his formative years of learning the Taoist arts on Wudang Mountain, someone in our group asked whether he and the other students ever took a day off from training to give their muscles a chance to recuperate. At the time, all of us in the group were hurting physically, due to the relentless 18-hour days of intensive Tai chi training and conditioning, so we were all interested to hear his answer.

Master Chen responded with a look of total incomprehension. "What do you mean, a day off?" He then went on to tell us that China was experiencing the chaos of a Cultural Revolution during the time that he was training, which meant that mastering the various Taoist arts was a matter of life or death, both for himself and the arts. In winter, for example, they practiced Hard Qigong (a strenuous form of internal energy exercise) to physically survive the cold. Beyond that, Master Chen felt that each and every day of practice and study was precious, because each day could very well have been the last day he and his masters would be around to perpetuate the survival of these arts and traditions they were charged with preserving. "No time to waste for a day off!" he concluded.

While I have paraphrased his teaching, that is the essence of it. I tell it to illustrate how easy it is to complain and find excuses to turn away from our commitments when our lives are relatively soft and comfortable. Most of us do not regard a daily practice as a matter of life or death, because for most of us in the Western world, it is not. So we find a way to compromise. Master Chen holds a very different viewpoint. "You cannot negotiate with Tao," he reminds his students repeatedly.

What I am suggesting to you is that once you have discovered a practice that nurtures you on all levels, remain clear regarding its benefits and how it relates to your purpose in life. Then use that clarity of purpose to overcome any and all of the ten thousand excuses to not practice. Find the deepest motivating factor for yourself as an individual, and you will never be the one to wonder whether you need or want to take a day off. You will know that every day of practice is more precious than any material treasure, because it brings you one step closer to your original self, one step closer to peace, and one step closer to connection with all that is.

When I was a student of Master Jou Tsung Hwa's, I would make it a point to thank him for his teaching at the end of class, and he would often say to me, "Observe nature; observe yourself; teach yourself." Over time he passed along many insights, each one a seed which, if cultivated, was sure to blossom. My hope is this book will serve as a reminder of your own inner wisdom and that I have been able to provide you with a packet of seeds you can use in the planting and cultivation of your own garden of peace.

May you always know peace, good health, and happiness.